Sprout Garden

Revised Edition

Indoor Grower's Guide
to Gourmet Sprouts

Mark M. Braunstein

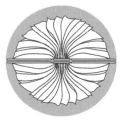

Book Publishing Company
Summertown, Tennessee

Front cover photograph: Mark M. Braunstein and Judith Summers
Back cover photograph: Mark M. Braunstein
Cover design: Warren C. Jefferson
Interior design: Gwynelle Dismukes and Warren C. Jefferson

Published in the United States of America by:
    Book Publishing Co.
    P.O. Box 99
    Summertown, TN 38483
    888-260-8458
02 01 00 99   6 5 4 3 2 1
ISBN 1-57067-073-0

Library of Congress Cataloging-in-Publication Data

Braunstein, Mark Mathew
    Sprout garden : indoor grower's guide to gourmet sprouts / Mark
M. Braunstein. -- Rev. ed.
    p. cm.
  Includes bibliographical references.
  ISBN 1-57067-073-0 (alk. paper)
  1. Sprouts. 2. Cookery (Sprouts) I. Title.
  SB324.53 .B73 1999
  635--dc21   99-14286
                                            CIP

Table of Contents

The smallest sprout shows there is really no death.

—Walt Whitman, Leaves of Grass

Foreword

In the early 1980s, although I had been a vegetarian for ten years, my reading Mark's book, *Radical Vegetarianism*, profoundly affected my life. I began to look at life in a whole different light, really appreciating all creation and realizing that every part of life is sacred.

I now have been a student of health and healing for twenty years. Embracing a vegetarian life-style, my mostly "living foods" diet consists of a variety of sprouts, fruits, vegetables, seeds, and nuts. You will always find sprouts growing in my home and, except when fasting, I eat sprouts daily.

Sprouts are the cornerstone of the living foods diet and, in my opinion, should comprise a part of any diet concerned with healing, optimum health, and vitality. These remarkable gifts of nature are pure, fresh, nutrient-rich, and alive with their vital force intact. Deeply rooted in the past with a growing grasp on the present, sprouts are the food for the future.

What food can you easily produce and enjoy whether you're 3 years old or 103, whether you're living in an inner-city high-rise or on an isolated island? What food is grown indoors with no soil, is harvested in two to seven days, and is loved by children, dogs, horses, and husbands alike? What can supply your family with fresh vegetables year-round, regardless of the season, while decreasing your food bill substantially? What food is simple to cultivate, produces no waste, is edible raw or cooked, and is delicious either eaten alone or included in an exciting array of recipes?

The answer is SPROUTS.

As a food, sprouts are 5,000 years old. In 2939 B.C., the emperor of China wrote about the versatile qualities of sprouts. Sprouts still remain one of the most nutritious foods on earth. The humble sprout truly is one of nature's most amazing creations.

Start with a small, dry, hard seed. Add warm air and a little water. New life emerges as if by magic from the dormant seed. Vibrant with life and bursting with energy, its tiny size belies the extraordinary activities which take place while growing. In a duration of mere hours and at a cost to you of just pennies, its delicate shoot proceeds to provide the most vital food imaginable.

Sprouts increase in nutritional content as they grow, especially in vitamins A, B-complex, C, E, and K. Sometimes the increases prove truly remarkable. The vitamin C in sprouted peas increases eightfold in four days (compared to dry peas). The vitamin B-complex in sprouted wheat increases sixfold and vitamin E threefold in four days of sprouting. Nutritional value does not stop there. Many different minerals abound in sprouts, and in an assimilable form, having been chelated by the sprouts for your body's immediate use. If eaten raw, sprouts provide a storehouse of enzymes. Simply from soaking, the enzyme factory comes alive.

All vegetables, nuts, seeds, beans, and grains begin life as sprouts.

Home-grown sprouts are the freshest, most assuredly organic food available to you. Few crops compare with "picking your own" just before you eat it and knowing it is free from fungicides and insecticides. When you eat sprouts, you are receiving the plant's peak nutrition, when nature has mobilized all of its nourishment to bring forth a mature plant.

If you seek greater health or faster healing, if you wish to nourish your body as never before, if you want to learn how to sprout or how to use sprouts in a variety of recipes, then *The Sprout Garden* is written just for you. Mark's is the most complete book about sprouts I have seen. Not only does he discuss all methods of sprouting, he also details the different sprouts, sharing everything you need to know to become an expert sprouter. What I particularly appreciate are the wonderful recipes using sprouts. Mark's latest book is as enjoyable as it is practical. I wholeheartedly recommend it.

Susan Smith Jones, Ph.D.
author of *Choose to be Healthy* and
Choose to Live Peacefully

Sproutarian Seminarium

Once upon a time some benevolent Greek gods offered to mere mortals all the sweetness of nectar combined with all the nourishment of ambrosia in a single source. Coming from a whole seed, it was half-fruit; becoming an entire plant, it was half-vegetable. One cautious god among them doubted whether humankind would appreciate the best of both worlds, and whether it even deserved it. The East immediately adapted this nearly perfect food into its diet. The West, however, procrastinated several centuries with experiments before its malnourished scientific community was convinced. That time is now. That food is sprouts.

Inside every sleeping seed awaits an unseen sprout cushioned by a nurturing starch and armored with a protective shell. With water and warmth the hard shell becomes soft, the soft shell drinks in the water, the watery seed swells, and the seed bursts. Happy Birthday! The root reaches downward and the stem shoots upward. Starches convert to simple sugars, proteins break down to amino acids, enzymes activate, and vitamins increase two to tenfold. Dry, the nutrients are locked away, insoluble and indigestible. Sprouted, a culinary key opens the gastronomic door. The dry sunflower that tastes like wood, when sprouted tastes like leaves. The cooked soybean that causes flatulence, when sprouted for two days and cooked for twenty minutes produces neither odor nor sound.

Sprouts are the easiest, fastest, and freshest vegetable you can grow. Their cost is negligible, their addition to any otherwise standard menu is delightful, and their nutrition is considerable. Sprouts are natural vitamin "pills," and mineral and protein "pills" too. But being natural, they are not pills. Need we repeat the nutritional evaluations of sprouts here? Let us only say that sprouts are good for you, and taste good too.

Do they truly taste good? If your first introduction to sprouts was at the steak house salad bar, you might think otherwise. Either the sprouts were overgrown and bitter or their succulence went unappreciated alongside the more familiar bleeding steak. Some folks eat the same foods customary since infancy. Yet they can just as easily develop the habit of eating nourishing foods as debilitating ones. Once sampled, sprouts can certainly become your favorite vegetables. Maybe your only vegetables.

Try an experiment. Assuming that almonds and sunflower seeds are already pleasing to your palate, soak them in water for half a day, drain, and eat them as they are. If you agree that simply soaking improves their taste and digestibility, welcome to your new life as a gardener and gourmet of sprouts. Grains, beans, and seeds that are both delectable to eat and practical to sprout range in shape and color from the concave lens of the brown lentil to the oblong sphere of the golden alfalfa seed. Everyone knows mung sprouts from Chinese restaurants, but how about sprouted rice? In a simple glass jar that requires neither sunlight nor soil, and with only an hour's work spread over three days, you can cultivate a choice of over thirty varieties of sprouts. You need not toil long and hard, sweating under the summer sun, defending your crop from insects and weeds. Yet you are fully assured that your harvest is organically grown, absolutely fresh, and utterly cheap.

Not since Adam and Eve caught the midnight express out of Eden were fresh vegetables so readily available as in today's supermarkets. Yet supermarket produce, chemically fertilized and pesticide-sprayed, furnishes only the façade of wholesomeness. Organically grown produce provides an unmistakably superior alternative, but it is not always fresh and it is rarely cheap. A head of romaine lettuce flown across the continent hardly compares with lettuce sprouts freshly harvested from a kitchen "sprout garden."

Despite so much concern about eating foods whole, few people realize that when we eat corn, for instance, we eat only its kernel and discard its cob, husk, stalk, leaves, and roots. A complete corn plant in bite-size edible form, however, is found in the sprouted kernel. Although kernels originate from an inedible larger plant, they compensate by rendering more food than do unsprouted kernels. Thus, the world hunger issue could be solved not only by "diet for a small planet" vegetarianism but "diet from a small plant" sproutarianism.

Meanwhile, the family corn and soybean farm has gone broke. Ma and Pa sold the land and retired to a condo in Arizona. Their son, who drove the tractor, moved to Los Angeles where he programs computers. Their daughter, who raised strawberries, became an accountant in Scarsdale where she raises 2.3 children. A tobacco corporation bought the land and converted it into a factory farm that produces carrots so devoid of taste and nutrition that donkeys no longer follow them on sticks. Yet all is not lost. Grandparents and parents, children and grandchildren, all can grow sprouts.

Sprouting is a triumph of field expediency. New technology does for us what we previously had done for ourselves, and our society encourages that displacement. However, sprouting enables us to regain control of a vital factor in our lives: our food. You might now be baking your own bread, brewing your own beer, pressing your own tofu, or simmering your own soup. You might have gained a reputation as the best cook in town. Though the appellation may fill you with pride, grander compliments await you. Until your friends describe you as the best sprouter they know, you will not have heard the applause you deserve. A chef merely combines grains and greens, while a sprouter creates them.

A sprout jar does not contain an entire universe, just a garden. Tend that garden for three days. As the seed transforms into a sprout, its birth unfolds the miracle of life, and its growth teaches us patience and gratitude. Monks of nearly all religions share in common the discipline of gardening. In the past, some East Indian rajas retired to small plots on their former vast estates and ate only food grown with their own hands. Few of us own estates, but most of us can find room in our cupboards and sinks where we can grow our own sprouts.

Sprouts

Ins and Outs

Botanically speaking, all nuts, grains, and beans are seeds of plants. Every seed can create a new plant, that plant a thousand new seeds, and those seeds whole fields and forests. This occurs naturally enough in fields and forests, but to initiate this in containers in our kitchens we must recite the magic word "germination" and wave the magic wands of air, water, darkness, and warmth.

So to get started we need:

> **1. The container**
> **2. Air and water**
> **3. Darkness and warmth**
> **4. Seeds, Grains, and Beans**

🌿 The Container

Almost any container that permits drainage and is not made of aluminum, metal prone to rust, or most plastics can serve as a sprouting vessel. Worthy candidates include earthenware crocks, flower pots, bamboo trays, natural or nylon fiber cloth bags, the many brands of commercial sprouting trays and kits, soap dishes (without the soap), tea strainers (without the tea), colanders, everything but the kitchen sink. On second thought, even the kitchen sink. In fact the kitchen sink is ideal. Just turn on the faucet from above, and watch the water drain down the bottom. Of course, you will not be able to wash your dishes. A minor inconvenience. So, . . . you may wish to compromise between the ideal and the real by placing a jar in the sink and the sprouts in the jar.

The most suitable and simplest container is the wide-mouth glass jar. After trying every commercial sprouting device on the market, most veteran sprout folks return to the basic glass jar. No one advertises it because no money can be made from it. The glass container can even be recycled from empty jars of mayonnaise, peanut butter, or tahini. Best of all is the flat-sided mason jar—what Grandma used for home canning. These are sold in houseware stores and in the houseware departments of supermarkets. By the dozen, they are remarkably inexpensive. Once your sprouting operation gains momentum, you might use as many as four jars per person per sprout cycle. If you complete two cycles per week, that would add up to eight jars per person per week. Be sure to purchase the wide-mouth quarts (liters), not the small pints or narrow-mouth quarts (liters).

Whatever jar you choose, it must be rendered drainable. You can perforate the metal cap by punching holes with an ice pick or hammering holes with a nail. The caps will soon rust unless occasionally lubricated with your favorite salad oil. Instead of the metal cap you could use cotton muslin, cheesecloth, or nylon stockings and secure any of these with a rubber band. The rubber band should be strong enough to keep the cloth stretched tightly across the jar's mouth and to assure that seeds do not catch in folds or slip under the lip. While these cloths effectively allow water to drain, they do not effectively permit air to circulate when they are wet. These cloths must also be washed thoroughly after each batch of sprouts. So the fabric covers are highly economical but not as practical as some other alternatives.

Homemade mesh sprout tops for mason jars are not only economical, they are also easy to make and use. Remove the lids of the jar caps and retain the rings. Purchase from the hardware store a small section of nylon, copper, or non-galvanized window screen. Use the lids as patterns for cutting circles out of the screen, and insert these screen circles back into the rings instead of the lids. As with metal jar caps, the metal rings eventually rust. By then you qualify as an experienced sprouter, at which time commercial sprout tops are a worthy investment.

Sold in health food stores, commercial tops fit wide-mouth jars. The more widely available tops are all plastic, while the super deluxe models consist of plastic rings with removable stainless steel screens. Both models come in different meshes, each appropriate for the individual stages and species of sprouts. For instance, the fine mesh is perfect for one-day-old clover or alfalfa sprouts, the large mesh for three-day-old alfalfa sprouts or any-day-old bean sprouts.

One innovation upon the glass jar and commercial top is the Tube that has a removable top and bottom. Both can be removed for better ventilation and easier cleaning. Be aware that not all plastics "outgas" (release some of their molecules in the form of gas). Certain plastics such as polypropylene and polyethylene are quite stable. If the container is manufactured specifically for sprouting, you can be assured that the plastic is safe, at least for you if not the Earth.

🌿 Air and Water

Just as you somehow survive breathing the smog of Los Angeles or drinking the tap water of Love Canal or living in the vicinity of Three Mile Island, so will your sprouts. The air and water harmful to you are just as harmful to your sprouts, but the sprouts will still prove beneficial to you.

If your tap water is heavily chlorinated, set it in an open container for one day or boil it for one minute. The chlorine will dissipate. Other so-called "purifying" chemicals are not so easily eliminated. You may need to filter or distill the water. Many excellent filters and distillers are available at some expense. Fortunately, sprouts can thrive on water from most faucets.

🌿 Darkness and Warmth

Here we need not discuss darkness as much as the cabinet or closet that creates it. The cabinet nearest the sink is best. Try to transport the sprouts the shortest distance possible. In the earth, they move only vertically, not horizontally.

Until rinsing becomes either a sacred ritual or a boring routine, keep the cabinet door ajar as a reminder of your little friends inside. Or hang something ridiculously ostentatious from the door handle: a dollar bill (to represent the money saved by do-it-yourself sprouting), or a map of Florida (to point the way to your Fountain of Youth that Ponce de Leon so vainly sought but which you can now claim), or a wilted leaf of lettuce (to remind you of the aged produce you previously deluded yourself into believing was fresh). You can even hang some sprouts on the outside if that is what it takes to remind you of the sprouts that are inside. Remember: out of sight, out of mind, out of sprouts.

In a shady kitchen or dark bathroom, the sink or dish rack is excellent for drainage. Anywhere else, provide a dish or tray to gather the water that drips throughout the day from the jar. A single sprout jar inverted inside a bowl works fine. A greater number of sprout jars, however, requires greater elaboration; even an old fish tank or a dish pan will do. Cheap plastic containers, unsuitable for sprouting because they outgas into the water, are ideal for drainage for this very reason. Insects will not exercise their right to freedom of assembly at this new watering hole. They will not drink plastic-tasting water. Neither should you.

Total darkness or subdued light is not essential, just recommended. Although vitamin C content increases in sprouts grown in darkness, the real goal is to recreate an environment closely identical to the great outdoors. Most seeds germinate beneath the soil, and no place gets darker than there.

Room temperature is the single most crucial factor in determining the growth rate of your sprouts. It also affects how often you need to rinse the sprouts. For instance, three rinses a day for two summer days yields the same growth as two rinses a day for three winter days. The desirable rinsing frequency depends upon room temperature.

If the room temperature is too cold in winter, sprout near a radiator, heating vent, or in the warmest room of your abode (which is often the smallest room, the bathroom). Some veteran Northern sprouters suggest installing a light bulb near the sprouts. Its warmth, not its light, is sought here. Shield the sprout jars from the light in such a way that you do not insulate them from the heat. Sound difficult? It is.

A much more effective device is a fish tank heater. These range in power from 50 to 250 watts. The smallest, 50 watts, is sufficient for a cabinet the size of a very large oven. Rest the heater on a shaped window screen that is attached to the top of the inside of the cabinet. For wood cabinets, screws will hold the hanger firmly in place. For metal cabinets, heavy duct tape works fine. Make sure no jar (or finger) touches the heater. This set-up will successfully maintain a cabinet temperature of 70°F (21°C) inside a kitchen with an average winter night temperature of less than 50°F (10°C).

If such a "sprout tank" is impossible for you to construct, you may need to limit your sprout repertoire during January and February to the big beans (pages 79-85) and grains that thrive in cooler climates. Winter wheat is not called winter for nothing.

If it's too hot during summer when temperatures reach beyond 80°F (27°C), those same big beans readily rot regardless of how frequently you might rinse them. Some veteran Southern sprouters suggest that the refrigerator provides a cool, dark environment conducive for sprouting. Rinsing daily for a week (instead of the three or four times a day for three or four days) does achieve limited yield, but it is probably not worth the wait. Instead, wait until the fall.

After all, local produce is most plentiful during the summer. If you adhere to the wisdom of eating what grows locally, the sprouts growing in your kitchen cabinet in the winter could be your sole fresh veggies. But in the summer be thankful that variety is available to you. Postpone your sprouting until fall.

✹ Seeds, Grains, and Beans

Mason jars and screens can be procured from a variety of sources, darkness can be maintained in any closet, warmth you probably provide for your own comfort anyway, water can be tapped from almost any faucet, and air (good or bad) need not be sought; air (for better or for worse) is just there. So now you have everything at hand except the seeds. To begin sprouting, seeds are particularly crucial. Recent studies prove that sprouting without sprouting seeds presents insurmountable obstacles.

Supermarkets sell few whole seeds and grains. Their whole beans are often irradiated or chemically treated to inhibit sprouting. Their untreated beans still hardly sprout from the infirmity of old age. If you try sprouting supermarket beans, you are likely to concoct only a soupy slime. Dead or dying beans may be low quality but still are food, so neither despair over nor discard them. Cook them into soup—exactly what they are sold for.

Garden seeds are dependably viable, but seldom edible. Seeds intended for planting are treated with fungicides and insecticides, which if eaten in large quantities amount to homicides and suicides.

And untreated garden seeds, measured by the ounce, are prohibitively priced.

The most reliable sources of viable seeds are the health food stores and mail order distributors. Among the latter, some even specialize in seeds for sprouting.

When sampling any new seed source, buy a small quantity. You might locate a bulk mail order bargain price for five pounds of sunflower seeds, but if those seeds sprout poorly then you've bought expensive bird seed. Never stock more seed than you will need until the next fall harvest. That five pounds of sunflower seeds is no bargain if it lasts two years. Germination rates decrease every year, particularly every summer. The identical air, warmth, and light that cause soaked seeds to sprout in a very short time cause stored seeds to deteriorate over a very long time.

Store unhulled seeds, whole grains, and dry beans in darkness, away from heat. Refrigerate hulled sunflower and pumpkin seeds, and shelled almonds and peanuts. The refrigerator is a big synthetic shell, replacing nature's smaller shells. Store all seeds in airtight containers, preferably glass. Most (but not all) plastic containers affect the smell of the air just as they do the taste of water. Particularly avoid plastic bags, because they do a poor job of keeping insects either out or in. Even within glass an indigenous brood of creatures may hatch. Think positively, assured that seed with insects is verified without insecticides. If you are a strict vegetarian and consider insects an unfit food, do not discard the seed. Feed either the seed to the insects or the seed and the insects to the birds.

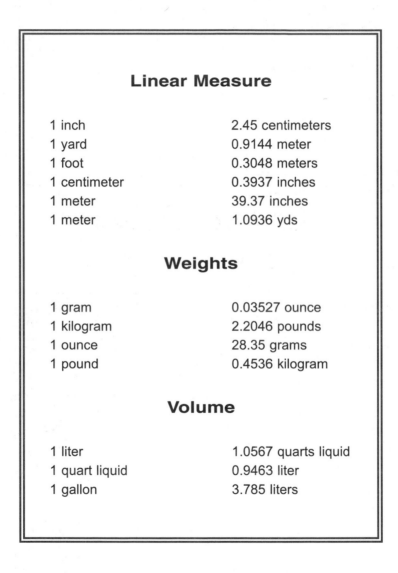

Linear Measure

1 inch	2.45 centimeters
1 yard	0.9144 meter
1 foot	0.3048 meters
1 centimeter	0.3937 inches
1 meter	39.37 inches
1 meter	1.0936 yds

Weights

1 gram	0.03527 ounce
1 kilogram	2.2046 pounds
1 ounce	28.35 grams
1 pound	0.4536 kilogram

Volume

1 liter	1.0567 quarts liquid
1 quart liquid	0.9463 liter
1 gallon	3.785 liters

The Sprout Route

How to Sprout

Count the stars stretched across the desert sky. Count the grains of sand spread upon the tropical beach. Count the seeds contained in a jar of alfalfa sprouts. Now try to count the many ways to grow the perfect alfalfa sprout. In order to conserve paper and ink, here are six basic sprout routes (which possibly total five more than you need to explore):

> **The Jar/Tube Method**
> **The Bag Method**
> **The Tray/Plate Method**
> **The Towel Method**
> **The Saucer Method**
> **The Soil Method**

The Jar/Tube Method

The most common container for home sprouting is the jar, and for decades it has proven to be the most effective. In time for the new millennium, a new contender has joined the symphony of sprout containers: Tubby the Tube.

While many nutrition books discuss sprouting in a page, they outline the Jar Method in a paragraph. At the risk of appearing complicated and confused, our instructions span over several pages. Not difficult and foolish, just definitive and foolproof.

The ten simple steps are:

> 1. Measure and cull.
> 2. Wash and skim.
> 3. Soak overnight.
> 4. Drain the soak water.
> 5. Rinse and drain (2-3 times a day for 2-3 days).
> 6. Sun (leafy sprouts only).
> 7. Hull (optional).
> 8. Cull and store.
> 9. Clean the jar.
> 10. Begin again.

We shall begin our bowl-by-bowl description with alfalfa sprouts. Granting that the seeds are viable, they will sprout even if your thumb is not green.

1. Measure and cull.

Measure two tablespoons of seeds. Eventually you will develop the ability to estimate quantities visually, but for now resort to the spoon and cup.

Pick the seeds clean of foreign matter such as twigs and stones. Extensive experimentation proves that stones do not sprout. Alfalfa seeds are too tiny, but larger sproutables should be culled of The Five Ds: *Decayed, Diseased, Discolored, Dented,* and *Dwarfed.* All these signify Dead.

Flat-tipped tweezers used by stamp collectors work best, but even a thumb (red or green) and forefinger will suffice. Do not deliberate too long over this. In fact, you may postpone this step until just before the harvest, when the quick are more easily discerned from the dead. In this case, a rotten apple seed rarely spoils the barrel.

2. Wash and skim.

Place the measured and culled seeds into the jar. Fill the jar three-quarters full with room-temperature water. Either vigorously twirl the jar or stir the seeds in the water with a spoon. A broad wooden spoon works better than a tiny metal teaspoon. Pour off the UFOs (the Unidentified Floating Objects).

Some otherwise lively looking seeds will also float to the top. These may be infertile, but you are wise to judge them innocent until proven guilty. Again, fill the jar with water and, if needs be, pour off the UFOs. Repeat this step until the water appears clear and the surface is free of UFOs.

(Using a Tube: Affix the solid brown cap onto one end of the tube. This end now becomes the bottom. The one and only inconvenience of the tube compared to the jar occurs at this step. The fit of the plastic cap to the plastic tube might not be leakproof. Test the fit by filling the tube with water before adding the seeds. If room temperature water leaks, pour it off and add hot water from the faucet. The slight heat will mold the shape of the cap to the shape of the tube. Next, pour off the hot water, add the seeds, add the room temperature water, and proceed as above.)

3. Soak overnight.

Just one more time, fill the jar three-quarters with room temperature water. Cover with a screen top, not a jar cap, because air ventilation is important even at this submerged stage. Alfalfa or clover should soak from 3 to 8 hours, depending upon the room temperature: the warmer the temperature, the shorter the soak time.

For other seeds, soaking times vary. A common denominator is 8 hours or overnight: a one-night stand. Let the seeds stand in water overnight, and while you are sleeping your sprouts will be waking.

Generally, the larger and harder the seed, the longer the soak time. When the saturated seeds have expanded to nearly twice their original size, or when they no longer rattle but just dully thump against the glass if you spin the jar, they are ready for draining. Be aware that the larger beans, such as chick-peas, or harder beans, such as aduki, might require 24 hours of soaking at cool room temperatures. (see Chart, pages 138-143) They should be drained and resoaked after 12 hours. If you neglect to change the water, the raw beans will rot in the jar.

4. Drain the soak water.

To drain the soak water efficiently, select the proper size screen on the jar top. Choose the widest mesh for maximum ventilation and drainage, but not so wide that you throw out the baby seeds with the bath water. For alfalfa, start with your finest mesh for the first two days, switch to a medium mesh for the third and fourth days, and graduate to the widest mesh for the fifth and sixth days.

Soak water is rich in water-soluble vitamins and minerals, so do not pour it down the kitchen sink. While bean water is unfit for consumption if you wish to remain sociable and comfortably silent, grain water and seed water are ideal ingredients in soups and sauces. Refrigerate what you do not use immediately or else it will ferment into a near-beer.

Feed all bean water or excess grain and seed water to your house plants. You will no longer need to provide them with commercial plant foods, most of which are either chemical or, if organic, are made from dead animal bodies. Your plants will thrive and thank you for it.

Incidentally, do not be concerned about the loss of nutrients in the soak water. Whatever is lost through soaking is gained back through sprouting.

(Using the Tube: For alfalfa or clover, affix the fine mesh yellow cap to the top of the tube. Turn the tube upside down to drain through the yellow cap. Now remove the solid brown cap, and replace it with the medium mesh green cap. The green cap is now the top—the yellow cap is now the bottom. A confusion of colors? Here is a simpler way: Purchase either two sets of tubes or an extra set of caps. You now have two fine mesh yellow caps. Affix one to the top and the other to the bottom, rendering either two tops with no bottoms or two bottoms with no tops. Either way, no confusion.)

5. Rinse and drain.

After draining the soak water, rinse the seeds, always using room temperature water. Cold water will shock the sprouts; hot water will kill them. Cool water will inhibit sprout growth; warm water will promote mold growth. Room temperature water! The question then is: whose room and what temperature? Answer: the sprout room at 65° to 75°F (17° to 24°C). If you live in an igloo in the Arctic, then your sprout room is probably a cabinet heated by a husky. If you live in a hut in the Amazon, then your sprout room might be a bamboo box cooled inside of a pit.

To rinse, run the water along the walls inside the jar (not direct-ly onto the sprouts), and fill nearly to capacity. Dislodge any seeds that stick to the top of the walls by gently twirling the jar. Allow the seeds to remain submerged for a few moments. Then invert the jar to pour off the water. If possible, lean the jar against the side of the sink to drip there for five minutes. That way most of the water will end up where it causes the least inconvenience: down the drain.

Water will continually collect at the bottom of the jar. That is why you MUST devise a setup to keep the jar inverted at a slight angle until the next rinse, 8 to 10 hours later. If you lay the jar flat, a puddle will gather inside. The puddle will cause rot. Rot will cause crop failure. Crop failure may cause the loss of one member from the ranks of sproutdom—you.

Small seeds, such as alfalfa and clover, cling together and retain moisture, so they require rinsing less often—twice a day. Large beans dry out easily, so they require rinsing more often—four or more times a day. If your schedule prevents you from tend-ing to the large beans every 6 hours, sprout them in containers other than the jar (see page 20). In the jar, decent results can be at-tained with minimum rinsing if you immerse large beans in the rinse water for nearly a minute before draining.

The rinse water of some seeds will appear foamy, cloudy, or dyed. This is sometimes true for clover (foamy), often true for large beans (cloudy), and always true for fenugreek (dyed). Rinse twice in the same minute when this proves to be the case. If the water still appears unclear, rinse again.

Sprouts are very forgiving. So don't worry if you forget to rinse them one time. But try to maintain a regular rinsing schedule so that you do not forget. If you work nine-to-five, a three-rinses-a-day cycle would begin early morning upon waking, would repeat early evening upon returning home, and end at night before going to bed.

Under most circumstances sprouts require only two rinses daily—all the easier. Eventually the routine will become habitual and will be exercised with as little coercion as meditation twice a day for some and with as much devotion as prayer five times a day for others.

(Using the Tube: Unless you replace one of the sprout caps with a solid bottom for every rinse, you cannot fill the tube with water, nor should you. Instead, apply the water, which immediately drains out the bottom, directly onto the sprouts. A spray nozzle works best; a gentle flow from the faucet or water filter is second best. Just no heavy torrents, or else the impact might damage the tender shoots of the young sprouts. Continue spraying until the water flows out clear. For the big beans, you can achieve the equivalent of a minute-long immersion by a minute-long rinse. If this seems like an excessive use of water, simply fill a bowl with water, and immerse the tube into the bowl. Two rinses a day becomes two baths a day.)

6. Sun (leafy sprouts only).

This step of exposure to light applies only to alfalfa, clover, and the other leafy sprouts: the easy-to-grow broccoli, cabbage, kale, radish, spinach, mustard, and turnip, as well as the more difficult chia, cress, and flax. All sprouts will eventually grow leaves, and all leaves when exposed to light will eventually develop chlorophyll. But such growth and development is not always recommended. (Just look what unlimited growth and uncontrolled development has done to the urban landscape.) The "leafy sprouts" here are defined as those we cultivate for their leaves intentionally, not just eventually. By this stage all the others turn bitter and tough, darkening the doorstep to your house of good sprouts.

In addition to all those alphabetical vitamins, geological minerals, and theoretical enzymes, leafy sprouts provide chlorophyll. But you must first provide light. So on the fourth or fifth day expose your now-leafy alfalfa to indirect sunlight. Avoid doing so before the third day, or the sprouts will dry out from the heat of even indirect sunlight. Sunlight is not essential, only preferable, and certainly economical. Full-spectrum plant lights are nearly equally beneficial. If nothing else is available, incandescent light will suffice. Even a bathroom window with northern exposure provides a fair degree of diffused sunlight.

Some commercial sprouting companies never bother to sun their alfalfa. They believe that the light the sprouts receive on the supermarket shelves, though fluorescent, proves sufficient. The faint yellow-green of their product will pale in comparison to the deep, dark green of yours. Simply keep your sprouts next to the window on the fourth and fifth days of a five-day cycle or on the fifth and sixth days of a six-day cycle. Even a single day is enough.

Be as attentive about exposure to too much light as to too little. If you supplement or substitute sunlight with artificial light on the two-day sun cycle, do not shine the light for the full 24-hour day. Give the sprouts light, but also give them night. Darkness, as much as light, is necessary for photosynthesis. As the eye needs darkness to define the light, the leaf needs darkness to digest it.

7. Hull (optional).

Hulling is optional and often unnecessary. Some folks skip this step—necessary or not—because they consider it one hull of a job.

Think of a sprout as being comprised of two parts: the living seed, which is the source of growth, and the hull, which protects the seed both before and during its growth. During sprouting, the hull begins to loosen from the seed. During rinsing, the loosened hull separates from the seed. After sprouting, the separated hull just gets in the way.

You might find your alfalfa or clover more appetizing if you deliberately rinse away the separated hulls. Or you might consider it less bothersome and more nutritious to eat the hulls with the sprouts. You know the value of fiber in the diet—the bran in wheat, the "brown" in rice. You can think of the hull as fiber and eat your sprouts whole.

On the larger beans such as soy, peanut, and chick-pea, the hull acts as an enclosure to keep the two halves together. If it is shed, the beans split and rot rather than sprout. (Try sprouting split peas rather than whole peas, and you will produce split pea slime, rather than split pea soup.) Naturally enough, the hulls of the larger beans shed only if you deliberately peel them. With alfalfa and other seeds, the hulls (not the sprouts) can rot. These hulls will separate from the seeds whether you wish them to or not.

Rinsing away the separated hulls from the sprouts might appear to be the most tedious step of sprouting. (That is why some folks skip it.) But several benefits are gained. (Which is why some folks bear it.) Your alfalfa will look more appetizing; dark hulls could be mistaken for little, crawling critters. Your alfalfa will taste better; dead hulls taste bland or bitter. And your sprouts will store longer during refrigeration; decaying hulls encourage bacterial growth.

There is more than one way to skin a sprout. You can do it little-by-little, rinse-by-rinse. Or you can do it all at once during the very last rinse. Or you can use the Tube, and let the Tube do it for you—precisely the major advantage of the Tube. Let us examine each of these ways.

Rinse-by-rinse: Beginning with the third or fourth day and continuing throughout the remainder of the cycle, affix the jar top with the widest mesh possible and flush water throughout the jar. Many of the hulls will float out the top.

But many of the hulls will not; they will float up, but not out. Keep the jar filled with water, thereby keeping the hulls afloat. Remove the jar top and skim off the floaters with a spoon. Stir the water and sprouts with the spoon; new floaters will rise to the top. Again skim them off. Repeat as often as this procedure remains productive. This will remain particularly productive for the other leafy sprouts such as broccoli, cabbage, kale, and turnip.

This method proves effective only if the jar is half filled with sprouts and if the sprouts can float freely throughout the jar filled with water. As the sprouts grow, you must either transfer them from the quart (liter) jar into a larger one, or you must distribute them among several other quart (liter) jars.

All-at-once at the final rinse: Transfer the sprouts into a bowl filled with water. Place the bowl in the sink in order to accommodate overflow and spills. Loosen the clumps of sprouts from each other. Then tease the individual sprouts apart, using your fingers as you would a comb or rake. You are combing out the hulls and raking in the profits.

Gently agitate and submerge the sprouts with the fingers of one hand. Hulls both will float to the top and sink to the bottom. Sinkers pose no problem. While pondering the exact theological implications of their opposing destinies, skim the heavenward sprouts off the surface of the water. Using your other hand, slosh and splash the hulls over the edge of the bowl. Bon voyage, hulls!

Be careful not to allow too many sprouts either to float or to sink. The trick is to maintain the sprouts midway so that they neither sink nor swim. While most of the hulls will float away during the first wave, repeat as necessary. Hulls will stick to your hands, so rinse off your hands as necessary.

This entire procedure, which may seem complicated upon reading, is really easy to do. Even large-scale, high-tech, computer-controlled, super-automated sprouting businesses utilize this manual method of hulling. The workers there wear latex gloves. All you will have to wear at home is a smile.

> (Using the Tube: Want to or not, know it or not, you and your Tube have been hulling during every rinse. The hulls have been draining out the bottom along with the rinse water. You can be particularly attentive to hulling by flipping the Tube and rinsing it through the other end too.
>
> For the remaining hulls, proceed as follows. By this stage in the cycle you will have affixed onto the Tube either one wide mesh orange cap and one medium mesh green cap, or if you have two sets of caps, two wide mesh orange caps. Replace one of the screen caps with the solid brown cap. The solid brown cap becomes the bottom, the wide mesh orange cap the top. Now proceed with the rinse-by-rinse method (page 27).
>
> You don't need to stir the sprouts in the water, however. The stirring is necessary only to prevent hulls from sinking to the bottom. When you drain the jar, the hulls at the bottom would be inaccessible without disturbing the tender sprouts. But when you drain the tube, the hulls at the bottom present no problem. Simply set the tube on its side, remove the solid brown bottom cap, and there the hulls are in front of you.)

Now you know that "hull" is not simply a noun but also a verb.

8. Cull and store.

If you were a farmer and the season was fall, this would be your harvest. But do not permit pride to fool you. You deserve every compliment and reward for a job well done, yet the work still is not completed.

The final rinse should always precede the harvest by at least eight hours. This step is so important that it warrants repeating.

The final rinse should always precede the harvest by at least eight hours.

There, now you have no excuse for not heeding this advice.

Never refrigerate sprouts that are dripping wet from the most recent rinsing. Such sprouts would turn mushy after one or two days, and moldy after three or four. If the sprouts are moist and you really must harvest them, somehow allow them to continue draining inside the refrigerator. Or before refrigeration, spread them out to dry on a white (undyed) paper or cotton towel.

For sprouts other than alfalfa and the related leafy greens, now is the time to inspect them and to remove any unsprouted seeds. A white towel provides an ideal background. Unsprouted seeds may rot or, just the opposite, may remain as hard as rocks. "Petrified" mung, guar, and aduki beans are the worst offenders. They will ruin an otherwise succulent sprout salad and may even crack a weak tooth.

Do not curse them as hardened criminals. Grin and bear them. They are hard, but also hardy. They are nature's insurance against the catastrophe of a late spring frost or a rainy summer flood or an early fall hurricane. If an entire crop of mung plants were destroyed before reaching fruition, it would not spell doom for the mung bean as a species. The hardened beans that did not sprout this spring would wait instead to sprout next spring.

Culled or not, hard or soft, dry or moist, mature sprouts are ready either for immediate consumption or for intermediary refrigeration. Nip them in the bud. Storage in the very coldest part of the fridge will inhibit further growth. Storage in only moderate cold will allow some growth. Even if they do not know whether they are coming or growing, alfalfa or clover sprouts will retain peak freshness for at least a week. Buckwheat or cabbage spoil within three days, which explains why they are never marketed commercially.

The fridge is just the larger container into which you place the smaller container filled with sprouts. That smaller container could be the very jar in which the sprouts grew, as long as it is dry inside. Remove the sprout cap and replace it with the original lid and ring of the mason jar. If you have a commercial sprout cap, a jar cap can usually snap right onto it, in which case you don't need to remove it. Or you can leave the sprout cap on just as it is, allowing for ventilation to dry out the sprouts.

Better still, remove the sprouts and transfer them into a dry "fresh" jar. Alfalfa sprouts usually pack tightly into the sprout jar, so you will need to pull them out with your fingers. For all the other varieties of sprouts, however, have another wide-mouth storage jar ready. Place the two jar tops together, the storage jar upside-down and atop the sprout jar. Clasp the two jars together with your hands and gently, very gently, invert them, and watch the sprouts tumble into your storage jar.

Some sprouts will cling to the walls of the sprout jar. Among them will be many unsprouted seeds (in fact, the "unsprouts" will predominate). This affords you the opportunity for automatic culling. Simply rinse out all the clingers into tonight's soup, into the bird feeder, or into the compost heap.

In addition to the benefit of automatic culling, the transfer from sprout jar to storage jar allows you to free the sprout jar from early retirement in the fridge. Instead, put it right back to work on the sprout route, the round-trip of many happy returns.

> (Using the Tube: No need to pull out alfalfa. Just open the tube at both ends, and push out the sprouts. The clump retains the shape of the tube and forms a very appetizing sprout loaf. All of the other sprouts will tumble out with greater ease. In contrast to the curvature at the neck of the jar, the tube is flat and straight—no bottleneck.)

9. Clean the jar.

Wash and dry the sprouting jar between each batch. Occasionally clean it with soap or sanitize it with vinegar. Residue from soap or vinegar can inhibit the growth of the next batch of sprouts, so use either of these sparingly and rinse the jar thoroughly. Avoid the use of bleach. It is bad for the lungs, bad for the skin, and bad for the beautiful planet Earth.

Actually, mere scrubbing and rinsing and drying are sufficient. The trick is to allow the jar to dry fully. If possible, dry it in sunlight next to a window, if not outside the window. The sun is a very powerful, natural fungicide, while fresh air prevents mold in the first place. Between batches, store the jar opened and in the open. "Fresh air and sunlight"—doctor's orders.

10. Begin again.

Time now to begin again. You may have fresh sprouts today but may be fresh out of sprouts tomorrow. And if you did not perfectly sprout your alfalfa for tonight, so what if your meal consists of second-rate sprouts? That is better than none at all. Because time prohibits the luxury of a second try for today, disappointment serves as a powerful incentive to do better tomorrow.

Sprouting may seem tedious at first and at worst laborious. But persevere and you will reap a reward that is both immediate and deserved. Sprouting is not an art, not a talent, and not a secret. Sprouting is a skill, a skill that anyone can perfect with experience. The great care you invest in this week's batch will enable you to devote less care on next week's. The question is not how long to soak or to sprout or to sun all alfalfa, but how to tend to the particular batch at hand. Experience will teach you when a next step should begin and when a batch has reached its peak.

As a novice, you may misjudge the signs, but soon enough you will sprout batches of memorable perfection. Until then, however, mediocrity may cause undue alarm. Be aware that the preceding instructions took into account the worst of all circumstances. Yours would be rare misfortune to come to grips with just one of them. (The preceding instructions also aimed for the best of all circumstances. Yours would be great fortune to achieve every one of them.)

Tending sprouts should be a joy, not a chore. Grow them knowing you are being good to them, and thank them, knowing they will be good for you.

🌿 **Notes** 🌿

The Bag Method

A popular myth exists that sprouting can be done anywhere, ranging from a backpack hike down the Grand Canyon to a midnight ride in the back seat of Grandpa's Chevy. While sprouting can be done anywhere, the myth is that anyone would want to go to such extremes. For such a daring individual, the Bag Method is ideal. And yes, it also works well in Grandma's kitchen.

Second in popularity to the Jar/Tube Method, the Bag Method is even more low-tech. You can make a sprouter out of a jar, but can you make the jar? You can make a sprout bag even if you cannot sew.

Bag Method—Construction

For a quart (liter) capacity sprout bag, start with one square foot (1000 sq. cm) or slightly more of loosely woven cotton, hemp, or linen. Linen (also called flax fiber) is sold in fabric shops, art stores, or canvas suppliers for painters. Place seed into the center of the cloth and join the corners to form a bag. Secure the bag shut with string or a rubber band. When the sprouts are mature, open the bag.

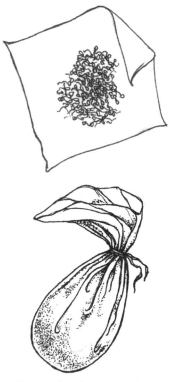

If you are ambitious and can sew, construct a more convenient bag by first folding the same cloth in half. Sew together the open long side and one of the two short sides. Then sew a casing around the open end for a string (like you would for a curtain rod when making curtains), tie the open end, or fasten it with a rubber band.

Commercial sprout bags were previously made from cotton, nylon, or plastic netting. The bag now most widely available is made from linen, and for good reason: linen, along with hemp, seems to work best. Although it is confusingly called a flax seed bag, it is not intended to sprout flax seeds nor is it made from flax seeds. Rather, it is made from the flax plant that bears flax seeds. While the cost of the commercial flax "seed" bag may seem prohibitive, the instructions that accompany the bag might prove definitive.

Bag Method—Sprouting Instructions

Soak the seeds either in a jar or in the bag placed in a jar. Rinse either by running water through the bag or by dunking the bag into water in a bowl or jar. Hang the bag to drain over the sink or into a bowl. During comfortably warm weather, the extra ventilation from all sides is an asset, but during intolerably hot or dry weather, the ventilation can be troublesome. At these times, place the sprout bag into a plastic bag in order to retain moisture. Perforate the plastic bag at the bottom to allow for drainage. Thoroughly scrub and dry the sprout bag after every harvest.

Bag Method—Precautions

Sprouts are fragile and easily bruised, so handle the bag with care. While the sprout bag is ideal for beans, particularly the larger beans such as pea or soy, it is ineffectual for small seeds and the leafy greens like alfalfa or clover. Never mind that these seeds need light; the real problem is their tiny rootlets anchor into the mesh of the bag. Even grains such as wheat or rye will snag in the bag.

As a solution to the bag snag, Steve Meyerowitz, developer of the commercial linen bag, suggests massaging the sprouts in the bag when rinsing or dunking. Just observe the first precaution: Sprouts are fragile and easily bruised, and the bag should be handled with care.

The Tray/Plate Method

The tray method, a standard among professionals, is increasingly popular at home too. It is ideal for growing alfalfa or clover and works adequately for the other green leafy sprouts. Trays offer one clear advantage over jars, tubes, and bags. Sprouts grow vertically in trays the same as in the earth, reaching for the sky or at least the ceiling.

Every sprout yearns to arrange itself consistently top up and bottom down. The tray enables the sprout to fulfill its destiny. With its chin up and its leaf standing tall, the sprout gains greater air circulation, with less chance for mold. Exposed to light, every leafy top develops rich green chlorophyll, the picture of health that is wealth.

When a friend first showed me her home-grown tray of bountifully green clover sprouts, I immediately fell in love both with her and with the tray method. Take away the "c" from "clover" and what do you expect?

🌿 Seedling Tray 🌿

Construction

Of all of the methods for constructing trays for sprouting, let me suggest the easiest to make.

From a gardening store buy two plastic seedling trays and one matching transparent plastic top. Large stores will stock a variety of sizes; small stores may offer only one size: 10" x 20" (25 x 50 cm). That happens to be the preferred size for really serious sprouting, but start with a smaller size if you have the choice.

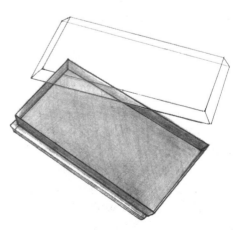

Now for construction or, more accurately, destruction.

Place the two trays together, one inside the other. One alone is sufficient, but two provide greater rigidity. The trays are manufactured with solid bottoms and indentations to puncture for drainage holes, if desired. Do so desire. A knife works well because it makes a long slit, which neither hulls nor rootlets can clog. Don't be timid; go ahead—deliver some good punches throughout the length of the tray.

On one end, at the tray's very edge, really jab away to your heart's content. Water needs to flow through here rather than just drip. This edge will rest on the surface when you elevate the other end. A gentle slope will assure constant drainage.

Now place the transparent plastic top onto the seedling tray. No plastic top? A sheet of plastic wrap will do. Voilà, one sprout tray.

Seedling Tray—Sprouting Instructions

Begin your green leafy sprouts in a jar or tube. Sprout them for three days in darkness. At the stage when you expose them to light, wash away the hulls according to the instructions listed in the Jar/Tube Method (page 27). Remove the sprouts from the jar or tube, and transfer them to the tray. Spread them evenly over the tray except at the two ends, which should remain empty for drainage.

Cover the tray with its matching clear plastic top. Set the tray next to a window or under a plant light. Elevate the end without the drainage holes. A small block of wood or anything equally primitive works fine.

For a really succulent sprout, rinse the tray twice a day over the sink. Water is an inexpensive ingredient; no point in being stingy with it.

Slant the tray at nearly a 45-degree angle, resting the punched end of the tray in the sink with its opposite end extending out of the sink. The incline assures immediate drainage. Rinse the sprouts with a hose sprayer if your sink is equipped with one or with a watering can equipped with a sprinkler head.

Clover and alfalfa are hardy and can withstand complete soaking from above with little chance of mold. But the other leafy greens, such as broccoli, cabbage, turnip, radish, mustard, lettuce, spinach, and kale, are another matter. If densely packed and drenched, their stems will rot. So spray only the top edge of the tray which was left empty of sprouts. Allow the water to trickle down the floor of the tray where only the roots will contact the water.

After spraying, leave the dripping tray in the sink for at least five minutes so that puddles collect in the sink. After the tray is completely drained, place it on a shelf next to a window or under a plant light.

Three days of light and three nights of darkness later yours will be the greenest sprouts in the neighborhood (unless we live in the same neighborhood).

To remove the remaining hulls of clover and alfalfa, grab handfuls of sprouts by the roots and dunk only the top leaves in a bowl of water. You should do this a half day before harvest. Shake vigorously while the hulls float away. Return the sprouts to the tray to dry out for half a day, and then refrigerate.

Hull removal in this way unfortunately disrupts the solid bed of beautiful sprouts. You might wish instead to leave the bed intact. Its sight is worthy of the praise of poets and the meditations of philosophers. You cannot have your sprouts and eat them too, but you can have them until you eat them. Cover the tray with its plastic top, and store intact in the fridge. Then remove the sprouts from one end as you want them. It's guaranteed you will want them often. Green leafy sprouts grown this way taste as delicious as they look.

🌿 Bamboo Plate 🌿

Construction

The bamboo plate is a variation of the seedling tray. In search of a more perfect sprouter, Steve Meyerowitz of Sprout House conceived of sprouting in bamboo baskets. Both plates and baskets, imported from Asia, can be purchased from Oriental food markets or gift shops. During picnic season, supermarkets and patio furniture stores sell bamboo plates as supports for paper plates. The more readily available plates are discussed here.

Place a ceramic or plastic plate underneath the bamboo plate, and a glass plate or clear plastic tray on top. Voilà, another sprout tray.

Bamboo Plate—Sprouting Instructions

As a variation of the seedling tray, the bamboo plate works in the same manner except that the rootlets will slightly anchor into the weave of the bamboo. This can be a disadvantage when you are cleaning the plate but can be an advantage when you are watering the sprouts and rinsing their hulls.

To water the sprouts, fill the ceramic or plastic plate that you placed underneath the bamboo plate with water. Allow the roots to soak for several seconds, lift up the bamboo plate, dump the water, and replace the bamboo plate.

To float away the hulls of clover or alfalfa, just hold the plate with your thumb on the bottom and four fingers on top, turn the plate upside down, and dunk the top leaves in a bowl of water. Thus you have not disrupted the solid bed of beautiful sprouts. (Thank you, Steve Meyerowitz, for a thing of beauty.)

ᚱ Combination Tray/Bamboo Plate ᚖ

Construction

Two standard-size 10-inch (25 cm) diameter plates fit perfectly inside a standard-size 10- x 20-inch (25 x 50 cm) seedling tray, which in this case should be left unpunctured. This is the best of both worlds. Enough said!

Tray/Bamboo Plate—Sprouting Instructions

Fill the unpunctured tray with water, lift up the plates, dump the water, and replace the plates.

Tray/Bamboo Plate—General Precautions

The seedling tray generates few problems. The bamboo plate, however, can have some quirks.

The plate is ideal for earlier stages of growth. But during later stages the sprouts will be crushed by any cover heavier than plastic unless you have placed the bamboo plate into the seedling tray. During the last two days, uncover the plate if it is not already inside a seedling tray. Either insert it into a large, clear plastic bag opened at one end, or leave the tray completely uncovered and just rinse it more often.

Upon harvest, the sprouts leave behind rootlets and hulls as souvenirs. Soak the entire plate and really scrub it. Then allow the plate to dry. Remaining rootlets and hulls can be brushed off when dry. The soaking and scrubbing will eventually wear away the plate, but being bamboo, it is easily composted and cheaply replaced.

❧ Notes ❧

The Towel Method

The towel method succeeds where all other methods might fail, especially for finicky sprouts such as the larger beans, whole but hull-less oats, and the mucilaginous seeds (chia, flax, psyllium, etc.). The towel is the best method to persuade the shy shelled almond to sprout. So just when you abandon all hope of growing such sprouts, throw in the towel.

Towel Method—Construction

While somewhat cumbersome, the "towel rack" is easy to assemble. Start with an undyed white cotton towel. The sprouts will likely stain the towel, so an old one is a good choice. Linen or hemp, suitable for the Bag Method, can also be used as a towel.

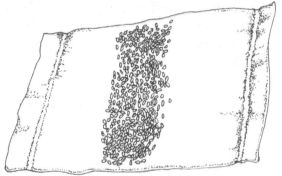

Moisten the towel so that it is thoroughly wet, though not dripping. Place the towel on a large plate or serving tray about one-third the size of the towel.

Large beans should have been soaked for 12 hours, almonds for at least 4 hours, but "mucil" seeds no longer than 2 minutes. Spread a single layer of pre-sprouts evenly onto the middle third of the towel. None of the seeds should be touching each other. Fold over one flap of the towel so that it covers the full surface of the seeds. Then fold the remaining flap over that.

During hot, dry weather, a second inverted plate or pan over the towel may be necessary to retain moisture. This creates a "Sprout Sauna."

Towel Method—Sprouting Instructions

Once a day, unfold the top two flaps to mist or spray the sprouts. Do not disturb the bottom portion of the towel that the sprouts rest on. You might damage the delicate rootlets, particularly of the big beans.

Almonds and oats are ready to harvest on the second day, regardless of how few grew rootlets. They have a low germination rate, and the ungerminated ones will spoil if left longer. Big beans and mucil seeds can be harvested in three days.

If you intend to grow leaves and green the mucil seeds, either transfer the sprouts on the third day from the Towel Method to the Saucer Method (pages 41-43), or better yet, begin them with the Saucer Method originally.

After all varieties of sprouts are removed from the towel, rinse the sprouts and launder the towel.

Towel Method—Precautions

Unwelcome guests such as bacteria or mold can grow in moist towels, especially if the towels are covered as in a Sprout Sauna. Bacteria and mold cause sprouts to rot, so keep a watchful eye for unwelcome guests.

Finally, when successfully sprouted, the mucil seeds can stick to the towel and be very tedious to remove. To help prevent this, first spread the seeds onto a nylon net or fiberglass screen, and place the net or screen on the towel.

🌿 **Notes** 🌿

The Saucer Method

Houseware and variety stores sell unusual animal-shaped clay forms for sprouting chia or cress. The sprouts grow like green fur on the animals' backs. One popular brand is called the Chia Pet (not the Chia Sprout). If you ask for these, do not mention the word "sprout," because the sales people will not know what you are talking about. The clay animals are marketed as novelties and gift ideas, not as food sources.

You can pay an arm and a leg for an animal-shaped neck and back, or you can construct a sprouter of your own for the price of a saucer.

Saucer Method—Construction

Look in your local garden supply store for a wide selection of old fashioned flower pots, the kind made of unglazed clay rather than the new-fashioned plastic. The unglazed clay pots are red-brown in color and are often imported from Italy. Their common name, "terra cotta" in Italian, means "cooked earth." Viewing the wide selection of sizes, forget the flower pots themselves and go for the flower pot saucers. Choose one between 6 and 10 inches (15 and 25 cm) in diameter as a starter. To convert it into a sprouter, soak the saucer in water for approximately 15 minutes, or until the bubbling stops.

Now for the very uncomplicated construction. Place the saturated saucer on a wide-lipped plate. Add water to the plate (not to the saucer). Cover the saucer with another wide-lipped plate, this one inverted. Now you have it: one Saucer Sprouter.

Wide-lipped plate

Terra Cotta Bowl

Wide-lipped plate

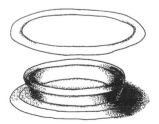

Saucer Method—Sprouting Instructions

Whereas the Jar Method works for all sprouts except the muci-laginous chia, cress, flax, and psyllium seeds, and the Towel Method for all including the "mucil" seeds, the Saucer Method works best for specifically the "mucil" seeds.

Temporarily remove the saucer from between the two plates. Place a small amount of dry (unsoaked) "mucil" seeds on the bottom of the saucer. The seeds don't need to be pre-soaked because the soaked saucer will provide them with all the moisture they need. Spread the seeds so that only one layer rests on the bottom of the saucer. You can do this easily by shaking the saucer as though you were a prospector panning for gold. The moisture will activate the seeds' natural mucilage, and they will glue themselves to the saucer. Any in excess of one layer simply will fall off as you tip the saucer.

Return the saucer to between the two plates. Now sit back and relax. After 2 or 3 days, change the water and check the progress of the sprouts. If the seeds are sprouting unevenly, seem dry, or their growth appears retarded, spray them with a mister. On the other hand, if they appear too wet, remove the water from the bottom plate for a day.

Continue to change the water in the bottom plate every 2 or 3 days. Sample the sprouts on the fourth day and every day thereafter. Their taste changes at every stage along the way, and this way you can decide which stage you like the best.

On the fourth or fifth day remove the top plate and expose the sprouts to light in order to green the leaves. (Consult the Sun Step section of the Jar/Tube Method on pages 25-26 for greater detail about lighting.) Beyond the fifth day, the sprouts thrive upon a daily misting in addition to the soak water in the bottom plate.

Their green growth can progress for another whole week, but of course, you can harvest them any day ahead of this. When you are ready to harvest, pull up the mat of sprouts from the saucer, and refrigerate them.

After washing and scrubbing the saucer, allow it to dry completely before beginning the saucer cycle anew.

Saucer Method—Precautions

The technique is simple and the result is beautiful. The only real admonition concerns the sprouts themselves. Their taste is not to everyone's liking. Psyllium ranges from bland to mild, chia from tangy to spicy, flax from pungent to bitter, and cress from hot like mustard to hot like hell.

🌿 **Notes** 🌿

The Soil Method

The Soil Method is an advanced step for both you and the sprout. Having graduated from Beginner Sprouting 101, you now qualify to enroll in Advanced Sprouting 202. By growing in soil, the sprout reaches an advanced stage, outgrowing the jar or bag the way a human child outgrows the crib.

The Soil Method owes its origins to the American sproutarians Ann Wigmore and Viktoras Kulvinskas. Ann first grew wheat grass on trays of soil in the 1960s. Viktoras expanded the cast of characters in the 1970s to sunflower greens and buckwheat lettuce. Credit for the introduction of pea greens in the 1980s, however, remains obscure. If not lost in some ancient text, proper credit lies buried in some tray of soil.

Some sprout folks never use soil for growing greens and grasses, employing other methods instead. Sprouts grown in these ways look paltry and taste bland compared to those grown on soil. By the fifth day, most seeds exhaust their own supplies of nutrients and hunger for those in the earth. Nourish your sprouts and your sprouts will nourish you.

Soil Method—Construction

To construct a single tray of soil you need two or three trays and some soil. This is advanced sprouting? What could be simpler?

Tray: The plastic seedling trays used for the Tray/Plate Method can be used here, except be sure not to puncture holes in the bottom. Same as for the Tray/Plate Method, double-layer one tray into a second tray for added strength. Instead of a clear plastic top, however, invert a third unpunctured seedling tray as a top.

The ideal tray is the plastic serving tray upon which cafeterias and fast food restaurants serve their meals. These can be difficult to find, but whatever your manner of procurement, obtain two trays. The second tray you will invert as a cover for the first.

Soil: The soil must be light and airy. The soil that you dig from your outdoor garden is usually second rate, because garden top soil is often heavy. It will easily repel intrusion by the sprout's rootlets, because you will lay the sprout seeds on top, not inside, of the soil. Even commercially packaged potting soil can be prefer-able. The best soil is fully decomposed compost.

Topsoil and potting soil both require the addition of peat moss or vermiculite. Mix one part soil with one part peat moss or one part soil with one part vermiculite. Heavy soil requires one part soil to one part peat moss and one part vermiculite. Mix in a large bucket to minimize the mess and to prepare enough soil for future trays. Add water until the compost or soil mixture is saturated.

Fill a tray with moist soil to ¼ inch (6 mm) deep for wheat grass, ½ inch (12 mm) deep for sunflower greens and buckwheat lettuce, and slightly deeper still for pea greens. Next, invert a tray of iden-tical size, and place it on top of the tray of soil. You have complet-ed assembly of your soil tray.

Since sprouting by the soil method differs according to the seed or bean you are using, below you will find sprouting instruc-tions by the sprout using the Soil Method.

Soil Method—Sunflower Greens

Sunflowers are likely to be your favorite soil-grown sprouts, so they might as well serve as your starter. The same freshly hulled sunflower seeds for the Jar/Tube or Bag Methods will suffice, though any chipped seed will rot on top of the soil. Due to their high risk of rot, hulled seeds may prove to be too troublesome.

Unhulled seeds are the way to go. You can choose between black (all black) and striped (black and white). Black sunflower seeds in the shell are smaller than the striped, and so are the greens they produce. The striped hulls stick to the leaves of the mature greens more tenaciously than the black hull seeds. Black sunflow-ers offer a distinct advantage over striped: a clear black and white issue with no shades of gray.

Forget sunflower seeds intended for bird food. These seeds are grown from hybrid plants that often produce inferior and some-times infertile offspring. The seeds might even be treated to pre-vent sprouting. Purchase unhulled sunflower seeds intended for human consumption. Contrary to the ridicule of your non-sproutarian friends, you are not a bird.

Day 1

Measure a maximum of 2 cups (500 ml) of sunflower seeds for an 11- x 21-inch (28 x 53 cm) seedling tray or a 13½- x 17-inch (35 x 44 cm) plastic tray. Both trays curiously measure approximately 230 square inches (1500 sq. cm). For trays of other dimensions, calculate a maximum of 1 cup (250 ml) of seeds per 100 square inches (650 sq. cm) of soil.

Place the seeds into a standard sprouting jar, and fill the jar with water. During soaking, the seeds float to the top of the water. Most of them stay submerged, but some will rise above the water like the tip of an iceberg. Unsoaked, these seeds will not sprout uniformly with the rest of the batch. You can remain unbothered by the small portion of unsoaked seeds, or you can remedy the situation by cutting a piece of plastic or stiff screen to the shape of the jar cap. Then insert the piece in the jar above the seeds. Press it down until it stays below the neck of the jar and the water flows above the seeds.

Soak the seeds overnight or for 8 to 14 hours.

Rinse them in the jar at least twice daily for two days as with hulled sunflower seeds (but no skins to skim off).

Day 2 or 3

By the third day, rootlets peek through the shells. Either on their first peek or before they reach a length of ¼ inch (6 mm), transfer the sprouts to the soil tray. If you wait too long, the rootlets begin to orient themselves downward in the jar, and it may be too late to reorient themselves downward in the soil.

Give them a final rinse, then gently pour the sprouts from the jar onto the soil tray, spreading them evenly. Every seed should contact soil, and no seed should rest on top of another seed. Do not place any soil on top of the seeds. The soil would cling to the greens, producing dirty sprouts. Instead, simply place an empty tray inverted over the soil tray.

Days 3 & 4

Set the covered tray aside for two days. If the soil is saturated (but not dripping!), you can forget about the sprouts. Take a weekend vacation. Sail the sea. Hike a mountain. Hug a forest. Your sprouts will take care of themselves just fine. If the soil was not saturated initially, you may need to mist it daily.

Day 5

After 2 days of slumber under moderate temperatures (or after three days in cool climates), the growing sunflowers will lift up the top tray, literally. When they raise the top tray off the bottom tray ½ inch (12 mm), you can peer into a vast jungle. You can contribute your share of the work by removing the top tray.

Days 5-7

Having developed in darkness, your sprouts now yearn to see the light. Follow the Sun Step of the Jar/Tube Method on pages 25-26. Indirect light is not enough. You need to zap the greens with intense light. A window with a southern exposure is ideal. You might consider taking the tray outdoors during the day; just beware of the blue jays and squirrels. They know a free lunch when they see one.

During the shorter days of winter, you should supplement even a southern window with a grow light. Place the light within inches of the greens. The greens will turn greener. Along with three days of light, allow three nights of darkness. Give the greens light, but also give them night.

Water the greens daily. Mist with a sprayer, spray with a nozzle, water with a can, rinse with a faucet—whatever it takes, keep the soil moist. But no puddles! If you overdo it, just tilt the tray over the sink to allow runoff.

Water the greens from above, not the soil from the side. You want the shells to get wet so they will become soft and pop off.

With intense light and sufficient water, the sunflower greens will pop off almost all of their shells. The extra care you take now will save extra work later (namely Day 8).

Day 8

Your harvest will probably fall on Day 8, but don't follow arbitrary schedules. Do not look just at the calendar; look at the greens!

Your greens are mature just before the second pair of leaves begins to emerge. If you delay your harvest, your crop will be larger and taller, but it will also be bitter and tough. As with great works of art, the great artist knows not only where to begin but also when to stop.

Be sure your last watering was the previous day. Dry greens store longer than dripping greens. Bring your ready-to-harvest tray to the sink for "dry cleaning." Briskly stroke your hand over the leaves the way you might stroke a long-haired dog. Most of the shells still on the leaves will now shake off. Where it is convenient, you can go outside to give them a fair shake.

Pick off the few remaining uncooperative shells. At last you are ready for your much deserved harvest. Cut the stems with either a sharp knife or scissors just above the soil, or pull out the entire plant, roots and all. But root pulling disrupts the soil for the secondary harvest.

Sunflower greens make a tasty basis for any salad. In fact, they deserve to be served as the whole meal. With a bountiful harvest you have the opportunity to indulge yourself. A standard tray yields more than four quarts (4 liters) of greens from the primary harvest alone.

Days 9-14

As a bonus, a secondary harvest awaits you. Tardy germinators, unawakened the first week, will emerge during the second week. The second harvest is not as abundant as the first. Repeat the procedure beginning from Day 5, starting with the light.

Day 15

After the second harvest, the Soil Method is completed. While all of your greens quickly disappear in salads and suppers, they leave behind a tray of stem stumps, roots, and depleted soil. Some idealistic sprout folks advise city dwellers to compost the leftovers indoors. These sprout folks probably never lived in cramped city apartments. The voice of urban experience instructs us to deposit the mat of roots and soil at the local park. The birds and squirrels will be thankful.

Country folks can set the tray outdoors for a day or two. Rabbits will eat the stems and remaining greens; birds and squirrels will eat the remaining unsprouted seeds. Recycle the mat in your outdoor compost heap. It's the best way to get a return on your deposit.

❋ Soil Method—Buckwheat Lettuce

Start with black, unhulled buckwheat. Hulled buckwheat is white when it's raw and brown when it's toasted. While you will not be likely to find unhulled buckwheat in health food stores, mail order sprout seed companies carry it. Unhulled buckwheat is a common cover crop, so most garden suppliers and all farm suppliers stock it too.

Cultivation of buckwheat lettuce is essentially identical to sunflower greens. Buckwheat is more fragile than sunflower and at Day 5 will not lift up the top tray as forcefully. You will need to exert a little extra effort and lift it off all by yourself.

Buckwheat grows a little slower than sunflower and might not be fully mature at Day 8. You will need to exercise a little more patience and wait one more day.

The only garden vegetable more beautiful than a full tray of mature sunflower greens is a full tray of mature buckwheat lettuce. Which of the two is more delicious is left to you.

❋ Soil Method—Pea Greens

The same whole green or whole yellow peas for sprouting will also prove successful for greening. Green pea greens: the perfect sprout for St. Patrick's Day!

Mold unfortunately can be troublesome. Forget about growing pea greens in the summer. If mold persists even in cool weather, sprinkle a thin layer of top soil on top of the pea sprouts when you set them onto the deeper soil below. Washing off soil from mature pea greens is more fun than washing off mold.

While all the steps for sunflowers apply to peas, maturity takes longer, nearly two weeks in fact. Forget any secondary harvest. The peas left over from the primary harvest will rot before the secondary harvest matures.

Some folks prefer to snip the stem just above the pea itself; others include the pea along with its stem. Unlike the pea in pea sprouts which requires steaming, the pea in pea greens can be eaten raw.

🌸 Soil Method—Wheatgrass

Sunflower greens, buckwheat lettuce, and pea greens all enhance traditional salads. Combined together, they serve as a salad unto themselves. Wheatgrass, however, is a different food entirely. You chew wheatgrass, but you do not eat it.

The same hard, red winter wheat for wheat sprouts works best for wheatgrass. Measure a maximum of 2 cups (480 ml) of wheat kernels (rather than 2½ cups for sunflower). Then, follow the same steps for growing sunflower greens up to Day 8.

You can harvest wheatgrass anytime from Day 6. The younger the grass, the more succulent the texture and sweeter the taste. If you harvest at Day 5 or 6 before the joint on the blade appears, the grass almost melts in your mouth, but then the grass will not grow back.

Generally, to chew it, harvest from Day 6 to 8. To juice it, harvest from Day 8 to Day 10. Once the joint appears, wheatgrass grows back after the first cutting. This second (not secondary) growth can also be harvested. In theory, wheatgrass will grow back after each of many cuttings, just like the front lawn that suburanites religiously mow every Saturday. In practice, excessive growths are neither as nourishing nor as sweet as the first growth, especially when grown on a thin layer of soil. Count on two growths at most.

Wheatgrass is more than just a green. Extensive documentation has convinced many health professionals to recommend wheatgrass. Its high concentration of chlorophyll heals and cleanses, but its fibrous cellulose is stringy and indigestible. To gain its benefits you only need to drink the juice.

One method of juicing is to chew the grass, suck out the juice, and spit out the pulp. Eventually your jaws may tire of the workout, and you may get tired of the pulp stuck in your teeth. When this happens, use a wheatgrass juicer.

Common household juicers are unsuitable because their high speed friction destroys the value of wheatgrass juice through oxidation. Wheatgrass will burn out or clog these machines. Manual food grinders are adequate but not optimal. The ideal machine just happens to exist, a juicer manufactured specifically for wheatgrass. Manual and electrical models are available.

❧ Soil Method—Broccoli and other Brassicas (Cabbage, Cauliflower, Kale, Rutabaga, Turnip, etc.), as well as Lettuce and Spinach

These seeds will produce a beautiful and bountiful harvest if you observe three very important procedures.

1) Spread Thinly: Spread the seeds or the three-day sprouts very, very, very (very!) thinly upon the soil. For the size tray that accommodates two cups (480 ml) of buckwheat groats or sunflower seeds, one-eighth cup (30 ml) of broccoli or other Brassica seeds is enough, and one-quarter cup (60 ml) is almost too much. Tiny lettuce seeds so densely fill any volume measurement that for lettuce even one-eighth cup is too much.

2) Water the Soil, Not the Sprouts: Tilt the tray, even at an angle as sharp as 45-degrees, leaning it inside of your sink as in the Tray/Plate Method. Water the top edge of the tray until the soil in the middle of the tray is soaked. Then switch the tray so the opposite end tilts up, and water again. When the soil is fully moistened, leave the tray tilted for several minutes to allow any excess water to drip out. Once the sprouts grow for five days, the roots form a mat with the soil. You then can lift the edge of the mat slightly off the tray and, even better, water the tray, thereby watering the soil from below, not above. One watering every other day usually is sufficient.

3) Harvest Batches in Patches: Sure, you can harvest everything in one swoop, but you'll not likely eat everything in one meal. Instead harvest batches in patches. Cut a path or two through the middles, one along the length, another down the width. This sort of "thinning out," a standard practice of outdoor gardening, bestows upon the remaining sprouts more "living room." Within two days, the sprouts in the remaining four quadrangles will lean into the open paths and nearly cover them. Then cut one or two new paths through each quadrangle.

Allow your checkerboard another day or two of growth, harvest that, now you're done.

If you do not observe the first two procedures, the stems will rot and your crop will be ruined. Observe these precautions and after one to two weeks the results will be amazing.

You will never again settle for such leafy green sprouts in their jar stage of three to six days nor their fully matured "produce" stage of two to three months. These one- to two-week Soil Method greens truly are heaven on earth.

If you have never before heard of these tender leafy greens, it is because until now no one figured it out. You read it here first, folks!

🌸 Soil Method—Experiment

Cabbage, turnip, broccoli, and the rest of them are not the final words in greens, just the Western ones. An entire array of Asian greens awaits exploration. Kyona (also called mizuna) is one favorite among many.

Likewise, wheat is not the only grain to grow, just the sweetest. Barley comes in a close second. Botanically, buckwheat is really a seed. You should experiment with other grains in addition to wheat and barley, and with other seeds in addition to sunflower and buckwheat. Clover and fenugreek grow successfully on trays of soil indoors. Finally, experiment with other beans in addition to peas. Any sprout that grows in a jar or bag can graduate to the tray of soil. Some just prove to be more practical and palatable than others.

Teenagers who join the Girl Sprouts or the Boy Sprouts can spend their summers at Sprout Camp. Then, in time for the millennium they, too, will become sprout scouts on the sprout route. They will cultivate new grasses and greens. And the very large and very hungry human family will graze from an even larger indoor garden.

There's Madness to the Method

In conclusion about the various methods of sprouting, here are a few cautionary words.

People who believe that their chosen method of sprouting is the only way should go dunk their heads in water. After soaking overnight, maybe something new will penetrate. A new thought or two may even begin to germinate. Like clover on the fourth day, they might just begin to see the light.

No one way of sprouting supersedes another. A boy grows soy in Troy differently than a girl grows fenugreek in Greece. And Amanda grows the same alfalfa differently in Atlanta than in Alaska.

Since 1971, I have tested every new sprouting suggestion in the books and every new sprouting device on the market. Some are expensive, but worth the price. Most are expensive, but not worth the price. The mason jar remains very inexpensive and very much worth the price. Indeed, I return time and time again to trusty mason jars for the bulk of my sprouting.

Once you have sprouted several batches with jars, you just may seek a change or a challenge. Please do try every method described here. Conceive of methods of your own.

Just remember that sprouts are conduits to both health and your wealth.

About Each Sprout

Sprouts are not created equal. Let's learn how to properly care for the different species of sprouts and how to promote their individuality.

The five criteria which precede each group of sprouts on the following pages are hardly the final words on the subject. Calculations are open to your interpretations. The criteria are:

Amount	**quantity of dry seed for a quart (liter) jar, tube, or bag**
Soak	**hours of initial soak period**
Rinse	**frequency of daily rinsings**
Days	**time to reap peak succulence and nutritional value at harvest**
Length	**growth of rootlet, stem, or both at harvest**

The wide ranges in SOAK length, RINSE frequency, and number of DAYS are contingent upon one other important factor: TEMPERATURE. Cool conditions require longer soaks, less frequent daily rinses, and more days. Conversely, warm conditions call for shorter soaks, more frequent daily rinses, and fewer days.

Higher temperature = more rinses for fewer days

65°F (18°C) = 2 rinses X 4 days = 8 rinses total

75°F (24°C) = 3 rinses X 3 days = 9 rinses total

85°F (30°C) = 4 rinses X 2 days = 8 rinses total

Now you get the idea! Whatever the temperature, whatever the number of days, the total rinsings remain nearly constant.

You can sprout two species of seeds together if you combine them with caution. Most sprouts require different soaking times and rinsing schedules. Some should be sunned, others not. Some must be cooked, others not. Generally, you can sprout together whatever seeds are grouped together on the following pages.

Sprouts fall into three general types:
(1) **Seeds**, (2) **Grains**, and (3) **Beans**. First, let's look at
Seeds.

Alfalfa and Clover	
Amount:	2 Tablespoons
Soak:	3-8 hours
Rinse:	2-3 times daily
Days:	4-7 (3-4 in dark, 1-3 in light)
Length:	1½-3 inches

Alfalfa seeds are sold in many health food stores, but you may have to mail order clover. Alfalfa and clover, as two of the three quickest growers of all sprouts (quinoa is the first), truly deserve the title "fast food." Remove half of the sprouts from a full jar of sprouts on the fourth day, and on the fifth day the jar fills up again. To sprout folks the magic word "abracadabra" sounds like "alfalfa-clover."

Commonly sold in supermarkets right next to the lettuce and tomatoes, commercially grown alfalfa sprouts compare poorly with home-grown. Indeed, the pale commercial sprouts are precisely the ones upon which the toxicity studies are conducted. You can revive the sad supermarket sprouts by rinsing them and sunning them in the daylight before dinner.

It's best, of course, to grow your own from scratch. For definitive instructions, begin with the Jar/Tube Method in the dark (pages 20-25), and then continue with the Tray/Plate Method in the light (pages 34-38).

Clover comes in red or yellow varieties. Yellow is cheaper but rather bitter, so sprout only the red (also called crimson clover). Red clover looks and tastes so similar to alfalfa that the novice can easily confuse both the seeds in the jar and the sprouts on the plate. Clover tastes slightly spicier, its hulls rinse off easier, its leaves grow slightly broader, and its green is deeper. Sprout clover once and you might never again sprout alfalfa.

Fast food restaurants have served alfalfa in their salad bars for some years now, making alfalfa the best known of all sprouts (outdoing even mung bean sprouts served in Chinese restaurants). Health food restaurants have served alfalfa as a sandwich topping, replacing tasteless lettuce or wilted romaine. In addition to their use as salad greens, alfalfa and clover can be juiced in fresh vegetable drinks and blended in salad dressings.

Alfalfa: The Little Rascal

A controversy exists concerning the possible negative effects of eating raw legume sprouts. Generally, this would only involve dedicated sproutarians, as most people take their bean sprouts cooked. The major exception to this is a sprout that folks don't always think of as being a legume: alfalfa and its culinary cousin, clover.

Legumes contain a variety of naturally occurring toxins, some which disrupt the digestive process. Researchers in India have studied cases where the use of chick-pea flour has been linked to an illness resembling lupus, an autoimmune disorder. Chick-pea flour is made from unsprouted beans that have been roasted, but apparently that process alone isn't enough to destroy the toxins. Cooking legumes or their sprouts in water, especially boiling them, does a better job. Some people feel that the natural toxins found in legume sprouts generally decrease as they grow, though not always immediately or completely. (It is also important to note that while some foods may contain small amounts of naturally occurring toxins, that does not mean that they are carcinogenic.)

Because of this doubt about these sprouts, some experts advise against eating any sprouted legumes raw. Although some sproutarians enjoy a number of raw legume sprouts, alfalfa is by far the most popular and, therefore, the most controversial.

As legumes, alfalfa and clover more properly belong grouped with beans, and beans should be cooked. Cooking destroys the natural toxins found in all legumes. Such natural toxins, when eaten in large quantity and with great frequency, may cause some problems. Alfalfa sprouts contain two toxins. Saponin can damage red blood cells, and canavanine can harm the immune system. Canavanine possibly had worsened symptoms in some cases of people suffering from pre-existing Systemic Lupus Erythematosus (S.L.E.), similar to the illness linked to chick-pea flour in India. The people in these accounts increased their consumption of raw alfalfa sprouts, leading doctors to think that canavanine, and therefore the sprouts, were the culprit. On the other hand, sprout folks who for years have eaten trayfuls of raw alfalfa and clover sprouts nevertheless present pictures of good health. Many guests at live foods health spas, such as Hippocrates Health Institute, the Ann Wigmore

Institute, and Tree of Life, actually have cured themselves of chronic diseases while eating raw alfalfa sprouts for the first time, along with all the other sprouts.

Saponin in alfalfa sprouts increases during the very early stages of sprouting, and canavanine levels remain constant until the third day, but both are reduced by *fully* growing them seven days, *fully* rinsing them daily, *fully* greening them during the day, and *fully* removing all hulls and unsprouted seeds by the last day. These toxins are water soluble, so you can wash your troubles away.

Cooking alfalfa sprouts to further break down any remaining traces of toxins is not a viable option. Cooking ruins their taste and crispiness and turns them into sprout mush. The one palatable mode of cooking that maintains their crunchiness is a very quick stir-fry. But some flavor still is lost.

As part of a whole foods vegetarian diet, such raw sprouts' substantial nutrients may balance or outweigh their potential dangers. (As part of a fast foods omnivorous diet, compared with hot delivered pizza and home barbecued steak, alfalfa and clover offer even more to commend.) Many other veggie foods naturally contain toxins. Leafy spinach and unhulled sesame seeds contain oxalic acid. Leafy lettuce and uncooked carrots contain nitrates and nitrites. You need not be fearful of these toxins, nor of these foods. You do need to eat a wide variety of foods in a balanced diet, and to eat any single food in moderation.

You may already know the first of the Delphic oracles, "Know thyself." But you may know the oracles only in moderation, because the second and less widely known of the Delphic oracles is, "Everything in moderation."

🌰

Advice, too, should be taken in moderation. This controversy over raw alfalfa sprouts was sparked so recently that its heated debate will not likely cool down anytime soon. Few experts seem to agree, so how can we? Let's examine the arguments of four such experts: two doctors (Weil and Cousen) and two nutritionists (LeRoy and Meyerowitz). Andrew Weil, M.D., is the wise sage and winsome guru of wholistic health. Long before his flowing beard and glowing smile appeared on the cover of *Time* magazine, his articles appeared in *Natural Health*. From his observation post in the November 1992 issue, he shined a spotlight upon the natural toxins in alfalfa sprouts.

Weil says that, despite its longtime and worldwide cultivation as a forage crop for farm animals, alfalfa has not been time tested or well studied as a food for humans. He does offer evidence that, as with any legume, alfalfa seeds and sprouts both are mildly toxic. So he recommends against eating any raw legume sprouts in any quantity or with any regularity. For those who want to include raw sprouts in their diets, he recommends the non-legumes.

Bob LeRoy, M.S., R.D., is a pioneer in contemporary vegan nutrition. He looks twenty years younger than his age, and he dances twenty years younger than his looks. As the nutrition advisor to the North American Vegetarian Society, he frequently contributes to their journal, *Vegetarian Voice*. In the Spring 1994 issue, he examined the controversy about raw alfalfa sprouts.

Since 1979, LeRoy cast alfalfa under a cloud of suspicion. He points out that some fresh legumes, such as shell peas and string beans, and some sprouted legumes, such as mung and aduki, have historically been eaten uncooked or only slightly cooked. Not surprisingly, the legumes on this short list also contain less trypsin, a digestive inhibitor, than other peas and beans. But alfalfa does not make this list.

LeRoy indicts alfalfa not just for trypsin, but also for saponin and canavanine. He assures us that among legume sprouts, lentil, mung, aduki, and pea pose less risk than alfalfa. And he further assures us that even if we eliminate alfalfa and clover from our list of sproutables, many nutritious sprouting options remain.

Gabriel Cousens, M.D., is the author of *Conscious Eating*, the definitive 1992 book on vegan nutrition. A magazine columnist in *New Frontier*, he addressed the alfalfa brouhaha in its February 1993 issue.

Cousens indeed advises against eating legumes either whole and raw or sprouted and immature. He emphasizes that alfalfa sprouts and clover sprouts can be eaten raw if the sprouts are fully mature and fully greened. In his clinical experience with thousands of people, he has never noted alfalfa or clover sprouts, when served accordingly, to cause any adverse symptoms.

Cousens reminds us to maintain a larger health perspective, to remember that sprouts and other live foods both enhance life and heal illness. Such foods contain a vast array of anti-oxidants, anti-carcinogens, live enzymes, vitamin complexes, nucleic acids, plant-based antibiotics, and other factors, some fully recognized, some as yet unknown, whose health benefits far outweigh the potential dangers of trace amounts of naturally occurring toxins.

Steve Meyerowitz earned the nickname "Sproutman" because he has promoted sprouts more than has anyone else. In his 1993 book *Sprout It!*, he gets to the root of the matter. He cites the scientific studies which sounded the alarm against alfalfa, and he counters that the alarm is unfounded.

Meyerowitz reveals that none of the research actually involved alfalfa sprouts as typically consumed by sprout folks. Sacrificial lab animals instead were fed alfalfa seeds and alfalfa hay, and only in two studies were monkeys fed alfalfa sprouts. Yet the alleged sprouts were grown fewer than three days, were not greened, and were not even served fresh. Instead they were dried. For half a year, half of the diet of these deprived monkeys comprised of only this alfalfa yuck.

According to Dr. Emil Bardana, the researcher in charge of this band of monkeys, "You'd have to eat a wheelbarrow full of alfalfa sprouts to get the dosage we fed the monkeys."

🌰

Alfalfa and clover sprouts were introduced to the human diet only in the twentieth century. The same is true for sunflower greens, buckwheat lettuce, and broccoli sprouts. The sprouts in our plentiful indoor gardens are the sprout stages of traditional foods with deep roots in the past of one ethnic cuisine or another. But not so for alfalfa and clover. One or two generations of primarily Caucasian humans is barely a taste test. One part of these plants at one stage of their growth have provided medicines or tonics, but not foods. These have been traditional foods only for farm animals.

Human digestion and human nutrition differ from those of horses and cows. I've never been so hungry that I could eat a horse. Nor so starved that I would eat what cows eat. (I chew wheatgrass, but do not swallow the pulp.)

Nutrition researchers contend that, among non-primates, guinea pigs have nutritional needs somewhat similar to humans. I can't vouch for what all guinea pigs need, but can attest to what some of them want. To research this, I confess, I conducted animal experiments.

I once shared my home with several guinea pigs rescued from the death chambers of the ASPCA. And I shared my vegan food with them. If they did not eat a food, then I learned to suspect that neither should I. In this way, I used my guinea pigs as guinea pigs.

Offered only raw foods, they merely sampled seed sprouts and grain sprouts, they completely devoured sunflower greens and buckwheat greens, but they shied away from bean sprouts and alfalfa sprouts.

My report does not serve as a clinical study, but gives pause for thought just the same. A good rule of tongue is to eat as sprouts only those foods whose unsprouted seeds or mature plants we also eat. Thus I have decided to be prudent and to banish alfalfa and clover from my own sprouting repertory.

If you too choose to spare yourself from doubts about sprouts, you certainly will not miss the very tedious procedure of rinsing away or shaking off the hulls from alfalfa and clover. With a wealth of possibilities from among dozens of other raw non-legume sprouts, you'll still have much to choose. You'll still feel easy, and like you're in the clover, without having to feel queasy about the clover inside you.

"Broccoli and the Brassicas"
Broccoli, Broccoli Raab, Cabbage, Cauliflower, Kale, Collard, Turnip, Rutabaga, Kohlrabi, Canola, Brussels Sprouts, Mustard Greens, Oriental Greens

Amount	2-4 tablespoons (4 tbsp = ¼ cup)
Soak	4-8 hours
Rinse	2-3 times daily
Days	3-5 for Jar Method, 7-14 for Soil Method
Length	1-1½ inches

"Brassica" is the botanical name for the plant family called cruciferous vegetables, called crucifers for short, and for shorter called coles, as in coleslaw. In the mid-1980s, they were knighted with titles of nobility as cancer fighters. In the late 1990s, the broccoli sprout (and by association the sprouts of the entire brassica family) was further promoted to the rank of "Cancer Fighter Commander-in-Chief."

Credit this to the laboratory pharmacologists at Johns Hopkins University's Brassica Foundation for Chemoprotection Research. In 1997, their findings were published in an article descriptively titled, "Broccoli Sprouts: An exceptionally rich source of inducers of enzymes that protect against chemical carcinogens."

All brassicas host phytonutrients, in addition to fiber and vitamins A and C, that guard the body against cancer. If cancer already is present, they armor the body to suppress further cancer growth. While phyto means plant, its pronunciation is strategically "fight-o." One phytonutrient is the natural antioxidant sulforaphane. Compared bite-for-bite with mature broccoli, broccoli sprouts contain 20 to 50 times more of this cancer fighter.

While worrying about cancer induces cancer growth, thinking about broccoli promotes broccoli growth. So let's just contemplate broccoli sprouts.

Soon after the above findings were publicized, fast-foodist Americans who previously ate little broccoli and few sprouts began embellishing their fat-laden but otherwise sustenance-starved diet with . . . broccoli sprouts. The 1997 world inventory of broccoli seeds quickly was snatched up, hatched up, and sold out. In order to meet the unprecedented demand for sprouting seeds, a few shady seed suppliers broadened their definitions of broccoli to include broccoli raab, cauliflower, and other brassicas. They sold these as seeds for broccoli sprouts until the enlarged 1998 harvest could render unto Caesar's salad what was truly Caesar's salad.

Such a ruse could succeed because the seeds of the brassicas all look identical. With some exceptions, such as red Russian kale with its red blushing stems, the sprouts all look the same too. They're all in the same family! Grown for more than a month, a cabbage develops characteristics different from, say, a kale. But grown only for five days in a jar or for two weeks on soil and in the sun, such sprouts provide ample evidence that if you've seen one brassica you've seen them all.

Their tastes, however, do vary. Even among different subspecies of broccoli proper, some sprouts smell and taste musty, others smell fragrant and taste tangy. None taste like mature broccoli.

Cabbage sprouts, though, do taste like mature cabbage. If your eating raw, mature cabbage leaves you with indigestion, you can eat raw cabbage sprouts without worry.

If mature mustard greens are too spicy hot for your taste, then mustard greens as sprouts will prove even less appealing. Mustard sprouts taste more like mustard spread.

Rutabaga and turnip taste similar as sprouts, which you'd expect of culinary cousins so similar as veggies. Varieties of kale sprouts range from okay to yummy, with red Russian kale the clear winner in the farms race.

Many Oriental greens of the brassica family, among them Chinese cabbage, bok choy (pak choi), tatsoi, kyona (mizuna), hon tsai tai, and garland chrysanthemum, offer weary Westerners an entire new world to explore. Even if you've tired of and renounced these full-grown greens, you can turn over a new leaf and try these greens as sprouts. Just don't try to pronounce them. Brussels sprouts sprouts, easy to pronounce, are rumored to cause speech impediments, though only temporarily.

Canola is a new arrival, perhaps deserving the same caution as for alfalfa and clover. Canola's forebear is rapeseed, the round black seed in birdseed mixtures, and Canada's former major oil-seed crop. Rapeseed contains erucic acid, which possibly harms the human liver, hence rapeseed's absence from the human food scene. But breeders recently cultivated a new, low-acid variety and renamed it canola (CANadian-OIL-A). Canola now is Canada's major oil-seed and a new oil for human consumption. Widely used as non-legume cover crops, both rapeseed and canola are listed in many garden seed catalogs at much less cost than any other brassica. Choose canola, and leave the rapeseed for the birdseed.

Sources for sprouting seeds usually offer broccoli, but few other brassicas. Your search for other brassicas will prove bountiful from gardening seed sources. Most garden seeds are routinely treated with fungicides and sometimes also with insecticides, so restrict your selections to only untreated seeds.

Small packets serve as samplers, enough for a single trial tray. Varieties within the same species that differ in taste as fully mature veggies will differ also as sprouts. After sampling, you'll want bulk quantities by the kilo or pound. Please refer to the Sources section on pages 120-134 for listings for untreated seeds in bulk.

Once you've found your favorites, stock only a few of these at any one time. Viability diminishes with age, so if you purchase by the kilo or pound, two or three brassicas should suffice. For instance, if you choose broccoli, then skip cauliflower and broccoli raab. Turnip should be enough, so you can omit rutabaga and kohlrabi. If you've got kale, then forget cabbage.

Now, how should you treat these untreated seeds? The Jar/Tube Method works best as a start. If you sprout them no farther than in the jar, be sure to green them for at least one day. But folks who sprout them only this far soon tire of the taste, which ranges from bad at two or three days, to bland at three or four days. For a truly delicious sprout that will rival sunflower greens, start them in a jar in the dark for two days, then transfer to a tray of soil as for sunflower greens. For further instructions, consult the Soil Method on pages 44-53. This all may take a long time to do, but with enhanced longevity, you'll have a long life to do it.

Lettuce, Radish, and Spinach	
Amount	radish and spinach 2-4 tablespoons, lettuce 1-2 tablespoons
Soak	radish and spinach 4-8 hours, lettuce 0 hours
Rinse	2-3 times daily
Days	3-5 for Jar Method, 7-14 for Soil Method
Length	1-1½ inches

First, a disclaimer. Spinach does not belong on this list. It really deserves no listing in any sprout guide or on any sprout chart. It nevertheless appears both here and elsewhere. With no explanation why it does, here at least comes the admonition why it should not. Its hulls cling tenaciously to the sprouts, even to sprouts grown for two weeks on soil and under sun. The hulls are too hard to eat, so they must be removed one-by-one by hand. Sorry, spinach! To paraphrase Popeye, "Even if I sprout to the finish, I can't eat my spinach."

Radish is easy to sprout, so resist the temptation to sprout lots. The sprouts are hot stuff the same as radish roots, so serve them sparingly.

The many, many types of lettuce compensate for spinach. Seek sources for lettuce seeds from the same gardening seed companies as for broccoli and the brassicas. Sprout lettuce the same way too, but with two differences. Lettuce seeds are so tiny that twice as many occupy a given volume, so measure out half as much. That's 1 to 2 tablespoons, instead of 2 to 4. And they are so tiny that if pre-soaked they stick together into one messy clump. So don't soak, just rinse them. Indeed it's best to skip the jar altogether, and go straight to soil.

You can use lettuce sprouts the same as lettuce leaves in salads and on sandwiches. Lettuce sprouts offer such distinct flavors that they can be the sole ingredient. "Hey, Gladys! One lettuce sprouts and tomato sandwich. Hold the tomato!"

Fenugreek	
Amount	½ cup
Soak	4-12 hours (but change the water after 4 hours)
Rinse	2-3 times daily
Days	2-4 (2-3 in dark, 1-2 in light)
Length	1-2 inches

Ground fenugreek seed is a primary ingredient in curry powder. Sold whole in Indian food stores by the name "methi," it is also sold in health food stores in the tea section. When steeped as tea, it is used for clearing respiratory congestion from the common cold. Indeed, fenugreek tea tastes like vegetarian chicken soup (though carnivores claim our memories fail us).

The dark brown variety of fenugreek seed sold for the tea is often old and sprouts poorly. It is also filled with more stones and twigs than you would care to cull. Instead, seek the light gold variety sold specifically for sprouting.

Fenugreek looks like large alfalfa seeds and sprouts like small mung beans. Both the soak water and rinse water stain deeply from the seeds. If possible, change the soak water several times. The sprouts can be eaten long or short, greened or not. They grow rapidly after the second day, so keep a watchful eye on them if you prefer to eat them short.

If greened on the third or fourth day, their spiciness can turn to bitterness. The chlorophyll may not be worth it. Try it both ways and decide for yourself. Our findings show three out of four sprout folks surveyed recommend unsunned fenugreek over all other leading brands. One favorite way of serving the sprouts is as a stuffing for a baked potato. The taste and texture of the two complement each other very nicely. Call the dish "Spuds and Sprouts."

Store fenugreek sprouts dry in the fridge, and they will retain their freshness for nearly two weeks, outlasting all other sprouts. Eat a large portion of fenugreek sprouts, and you too will retain freshness. The next day your body will smell like curry powder. Your friends will ask you if you have been eating Indian cuisine. Tell them it's Sproutarian American.

Chia, Cress, Flax, and Psyllium

Amount	varies—enough for single layer across saucer
Soak	no soak period
Rinse	no rinsing seeds; instead keep the saucer moist
Days	4-5 (flax 1-5)
Length	1-1½ inches

These four mucilaginous seeds successfully sprout alone only with the clay Saucer Method. Consult the instructions on pages 41-43 for a definitive discussion.

They will sprout by the otherwise trustworthy Jar/Tube Method only if combined in a portion of one part mucilaginous seed to four or five parts alfalfa or clover. Sprout the alfalfa or clover a day or two alone, add the mucilaginous seeds, and continue sprouting as you would alfalfa.

If you sprout these mucilaginous seeds alone, avoid eating them alone. They all taste strong and spicy. Be aware that what burns the tongue may irritate every other part of the digestive tract. The very hottest is cress. Flax, the least temperamental to sprout, is also relatively the mildest.

Flax sprouts and psyllium sprouts, just like their dry seed forbears, produce dramatic laxative effects: flaxative.

Sunflower and Pumpkin (shelled)	
Amount	1 cup
Soak	sunflower 2-8 hours, pumpkin 4-12 hours
Rinse	2-3 times daily
Days	sunflower 2-4, pumpkin 1-2
Length	sunflower 1 inch, pumpkin ⅛ inch

Sunflower and pumpkin seeds are available in every health food store. Seek seeds that are uniformly colored, unbroken, and fresh. If fresh, they will smell fresh—even through the plastic packaging. Otherwise, they have not been freshly shelled. Some sprout folks mistakenly believe that viable sunflower and pumpkin seeds are false rumors. Actually, fresh seeds are what prove so elusive. The seeds available in health food stores may not be that fresh.

Purchase yours either from sprout seed companies or directly from natural foods distributors. Store them in the fridge. All shelled sprouting seeds—sunflower, pumpkin, almond, and peanut—require refrigeration. Unfortunately, stores rarely refrigerate these seeds.

Upon soaking, sunflower seeds shed their coats at the drop of a hat. Rinse away the skins after the initial soaking and during the subsequent rinsings on the first sprouting day. Keep on rinsing. Those skins will keep on shedding. If you do not separate the skins from the sprouts, eat the sunflower sprouts rather promptly, otherwise the skins will soon rot and spoil the whole batch. Pumpkin sprouts shed no skin, but must be eaten immediately regardless.

Sprouted longer than two days, sunflower tastes slightly bitter and pumpkin absolutely vile. Sprout with proper discretion and you will deem these your favorites. The two are interchangeable in any recipe, if you use them in a recipe. Otherwise they are divine eaten alone and, of course, raw. Try them as sprouts once, and you will never again eat them unsprouted.

Sprinkle some sweetener such as maple syrup or date sugar atop sunflower sprouts, and you have created a delicious dessert. No other sprout deserves the title and rank as "Sun Sprout."

Almond	
Amount	1-2 cups
Soak	12 hours (change water after 6 hours)
Rinse	2-3 times daily
Days	1-2
Length	⅛ inch

You are correct. The almond is really a nut, whereas the peanut is a pea, not a nut. While nuts sprout in the shell (from where else do nuts come?), almonds will also sprout shelled. To spare it the loneliness of a category unto itself, we shall allow it to keep some seedy company. Its sprouting requirements are nearly identical to pumpkin seeds.

Begin with the whole, unblanched almonds, freshly shelled, of course! If you cannot find a dependably fresh source, buy them unshelled and shell them yourself. Almonds are the easiest of all nuts to crack.

With great care and delicacy you can succeed with the Jar/Tube and Bag Methods. Just don't jostle the nuts around too much. Even with apathy you are assured good results with the Towel Method.

Expect only a tiny tip of a rootlet to appear and on only half of the almonds at that. The sprout is rather shy.

The remaining almonds without the sprout are edible. In fact, they're better than edible; they are delectable and digestible too. Just from soaking, germination begins as almonds expand and soften. You need not continue the sprouting process beyond the initial germination stage of soaking. Admittedly, however, "almond sprouts" are much more romantic a notion than "almond soaks."

You might want to try soaking and germinating other nuts. Soaking proves particularly beneficial for walnuts and pecans. Their acidic skins virtually dissolve in water. You must change the water several times during the few hours of soaking or else the water becomes opaque.

You may never eat an unsoaked walnut or pecan again.

Sesame	
Amount	2 cups
Soak	2-8 hours
Rinse	3-4 times daily
Days	1-2
Length	¹⁄₁₆ inch

Nutritionists debate over which way to eat sesame—unhulled or hulled. Rather than choose between Heaven and Hull, let us say that only unhulled sesame will sprout.

Hulled sesame is white and oily, unhulled beige and chalky. As a garnish in other foods, hulled sesame provides some taste but slight texture and unhulled no taste but much texture. Sesame sprouts, on the other hand, offer the best of both worlds: both taste and texture.

Never sprout sesame seeds longer than two days. A day and a half is best. Otherwise, they turn as bitter as pumpkin seeds sprouted past their prime and gone to seed.

Next, Let's look at

Grains.

Wheat, Rye, and Triticale	
Amount	1 cup
Soak	6-12 hours
Rinse	2-3 times daily
Days	2-3
Length	¼-½ inch

Wheat sprouts are sweeter than rye, while rye sprouts are softer than wheat. The best qualities of each one together prove to be a good combination, which comes pre-packaged in the hybrid of another grain: triticale. In case you have not pulled your head out of the supermarket sand since the early '70s, you may not have heard of triticale. Equaling more than the sum of its parts, triticale contains more protein than either wheat or rye.

Everyone is familiar with wheat. Wheat means to the West what rice means to the East. Of all grains, seeds, or beans, wheat is the least expensive. You can eat wheat sprouts raw, so the savings on fuel costs makes wheat cheaper still.

Among the many varieties of wheat, the basic types are hard and soft, red and white, winter and spring. Hard, red winter wheat stores the best and is the variety most often stocked by health food stores. But hard, red spring wheat sprouts best, and its higher gluten content renders the best sprout bread. Fear not, you will still get good results with winter wheat.

Greenhorn and green thumb alike commonly sprout these three grains past their primes. Stop sprouting them before the appearance of the white fuzzy webs of rootlets, which are often mistaken for mold. By this stage, the grains lose their sweetness and softness. Store the sprouts in the very coldest part of the fridge, and eat them within three days. Otherwise, the rootlets will still grow.

If you plan on storing the sprouts longer than three days, soak them in water. Such soaking not only retards any further growth under refrigeration, but also softens them for easier chewing.

Wheat will become as soft as rye; rye will become as sweet as wheat and taste like wild rice. Call it wild rye.

The sprouts of wheat, rye, and triticale might soon lose their appeal if they are only eaten whole. To further prepare them, grind the sprouts into dough and sun-dry, or slow-bake the dough into wafers and breads. Sprout breads are also sold in health food stores, usually in the freezer section. Better frozen sprouts than baked flour! But beware the false advertising of the bread bakers. Many claim "sprouted wheat" when the kernels have only been soaked, not sprouted. These breads look like conventional breads. True sprout breads look like unconventional sprouts.

Rice	
Amount	1 cup
Soak	12-24 hours (change the water after 12 hours)
Rinse	2-3 times daily
Days	1-3
Length	⅛ inch

With 7,000 varieties floating around the world, rice comes in many shapes and sizes. We can simplify them into three: short-, medium-, and long-grain. Shorter grains sprout better than long, however, sweet brown rice often does not sprout at all. "Wild" rice, at three times the length of "tame" rice, is usually marketed cut and chopped, so it will not sprout. The best rice to sprout is short grain brown rice. The inclusion of the bran and germ differentiates brown rice from white rice. White rice does not sprout. The next wedding you attend, toss some brown rice sprouts at the newly-weds. With conventional white rice symbolizing fertility and fidelity, no wonder many modern marriages end childless or divorced.

Select short-grain brown rice that has few broken or chipped kernels. A green tinge to the kernel does not affect its potential to sprout. Rice sprouts must still be cooked, one part rice to one part water, for 15 minutes. This is one-third to one-quarter the cooking time for unsprouted brown rice. The real benefit is not time but taste. Cooked rice sprouts are sweeter than plain cooked rice. Thus rice sprouts are the true contender for the title "sweet brown rice."

Buckwheat	
Amount	**1 cup**
Soak	**15 minutes (yes, minutes)**
Rinse	**2-4 times daily**
Days	**2-3**
Length	**½-1 inch**

Also called kasha, the buckwheat sold in supermarkets and health food stores is roasted, so it will not sprout. Roasted hulled buckwheat is brown in color and earthy in smell. Raw hulled buckwheat, however, is white and odorless. (Unhulled buckwheat is black, odorless, and another story.)

Buckwheat, when cooked, is commonly considered a grain. Botanically, it is really a seed. Whether considered a seed or a grain, they both make sprouts. Not intending to cook buckwheat sprouts, we could classify them according to rules of botany, not conventions of cookery.

Even sprout folks think of buckwheat as a cooked grain rather than as a sprout seed. No doubt they initiated their only attempts to sprout it with a standard soak period of several hours. Therein lies the rub. Soaked buckwheat produces a sticky mess similar to the mucilaginous seeds quartet, unappetizing and unsproutable.

Buckwheat on its second and third days requires rinses at least twice daily, the same as for most other sprouts. The first day, however, is rather tricky. If you're in a hurry, you can soak buckwheat for just 15 minutes, and then rinse it 3 or 4 times the first day. If you have time to spare, you should rinse it hourly (yes, hourly) for the first 3 or 4 hours. The delicate balance lies between not too moist (sticky) and not too dry (tricky).

To prepare it as a raw main dish, sprinkle frugally with olive oil and season generously with your favorite herb or spice. This dish is worthy of vegetarian Thanksgiving dinners. Among an assortment of sprouts at any dinner, buckwheat disappears first.

Barley, Millet, and Oats	
Amount	1½ cups
Soak	oats 1-5 hours, millet 5-7 hours, barley 6-10 hours
Rinse	2-3 times daily
Days	1-2
Length	0-¼ inch

Like UFOs and ghosts, these three grain sprouts are often talked about but are rarely seen. Millet, barley, and oats are grouped together by common default. The unhulled varieties sprout easily, but the inedible hard hulls do not separate readily. The hulled varieties sprout poorly or not at all, because the germ gets scraped off with the hull. The former you can sprout but cannot eat; the later you can eat but cannot sprout.

If you insist on sprouting these grains hulled, rinse them often with cool water and only until the first grains sprout. Eat immediately or refrigerate the "almost-sprouts" before the remaining infertile grains rot. Keep both your eyes and nose on them.

Bare barley barely sprouts. You might not realize it but unhulled barley sprouts are a favorite food of our Pepsi and Twinkie generation, particularly on Friday and Saturday nights. Possibly before you ate mung bean sprouts in chow mein (and did not know it), you drank barley sprouts in beer (and did not know it). Unhulled barley sprouts are roasted into malt, and malts are brewed into beer (now you know it). To brew your own pre-beer, refer to the recipe "Captain Cooked's Sweetwort," page 122.

Rolled oats for oatmeal are dead and might as well be buried. Hulled oats from the health food store are often not whole but utterly cracked. Hulled oats from the pet food store, sold as parakeet treat, prove more useful. Oats sprout best with the awkward Towel Method; otherwise, oats are out.

Better news, however, arrives with millet. Purchase hulled millet from the health food store. Its 50% germination rate is sufficient. For a grain dish, cook millet sprouts for 5 minutes. For inclusion in wafers and breads, grind it raw. Mill it, millet!

Amaranth and Quinoa

Amount	⅓ cup
Soak	amaranth 0, quinoa 2-4 hours
Rinse	2-3 times daily
Days	amaranth 1-3, quinoa 1-4
Length	¼ to 1¼ inches

Amaranth and quinoa are like brother and sister. Both contain more protein, and protein that is more complete, than other grains. That makes sense, because both belong to the botanical family of seeds, not grains, but that's another matter.

Amaranth, though widely known, is not widely eaten. That too makes sense, because both the uncooked sprout and the cooked grain taste, well, lousy. The cooked sprout is slightly more appealing. To sprout it, be sure not to soak it, just rinse it. Amaranth is a sluggish swimmer that drowns in soak water. It's a sluggish sprouter too.

Like the Aztec amaranth, the Incan quinoa (pronounced "keen-wah") is a newcomer to North American whole foods cuisine. Unlike amaranth, however, quinoa is a speedy sprouter. In fact, it wins the competition for the quickest sprouter on the block.

After a single day you can eat it raw as a grain similar to buckwheat. After two days you can eat it as a green similar to alfalfa. Grain or green, its taste is accurately described as indescribable. In other words, it does not appeal to everyone's palate.

If your quinoa sprouts actually taste disagreeable, blame that on saponin. Quinoa that is the light yellow color of millet likely had its saponin removed. Quinoa that is the buff color of sesame seeds likely has its saponin remaining.

Commercial removal of saponin sometimes renders a low germination rate, so be happy for your "saponin a la quinoa." To remove it yourself, simply rinse the quinoa many, many, many times until the water runs clear. After that, you are ready to soak the grain.

The sprout grows nearly one-half inch per day for the first four days. On the second day, the stem turns red. On the third day, with exposure to light, the leaf begins to turn green. With the rootlet remaining white, the sprout unfurls its flag of red, white, and green. Quinoa may not be the most delicious of all sprouts, but it certainly is the most beautiful.

Corn and Popcorn

Amount	1½ cups
Soak	10-24 hours (change the water after 12 hours)
Rinse	2-3 times daily
Days	2-3
Length	¼-⅓ inch

Is corn corny? So-called "whole" corn from the natural food store hardly differs from cracked corn from the pet shop. The germ snuggles so closely to the cob that commercial shelling either removes or damages it. Perhaps half of all kernels are broken and germless, so these must be culled before sprouting.

Too much work? Then sprout popcorn. Popcorn kernels are relatively whole. Most batches will sprout bountifully. "Pop" corn sprouts, however, are not as sweet as "mom" corn sprouts.

You can attain a superior seed by starting with fresh, sweet summer corn. Shuck the husk, hang up the cob to dry, pluck the dried kernels off the cob, and store the kernels for winter sprouting.

After picking, the sugars in corn convert to starches. After sprouting, the starches convert back to sugars. The inner pulp softens, but the crusty hulls remain hard, so corn sprouts must either be ground or steamed. Steamed sprouts can be served as a snack popped into the mouth one at a time just like, that's right, popcorn.

Third, Let's look at

Beans.

Mung and Aduki (also spelled Azuki, Adzuki)	
Amount	mung ⅓ cup, aduki ½ cup
Soak	5-12 hours (some aduki 24 hours, but change water after 12 hours)
Rinse	3-5 times daily
Days	mung 3-5, aduki 2-4
Length	mung 1-3 inches, aduki ½ to 1½ inches (both before leaf appears)

Who needs any introduction to mung sprouts? We ate them in Chinese foods years before we were aware of health foods or began sprouting them ourselves. Years ago supermarkets only sold them canned, but now they offer them fresh too, alongside the alfalfa sprouts. Commercially grown fresh mung beans, however, are often bleached with sodium hypochlorite to assure white color and to prevent mold growth.

So grow your own, which is why you are here anyway. Some dried mung beans sold in health food stores come irregularly shaped, shriveled, and pocked with holes as though beads for stringing. These are poor sprouters. When you buy your seeds, visually inspect them to make sure they are regularly shaped and not shriveled. The dried mung beans sold in Oriental food stores are better in appearance and, though not organic, are excellent sprouters.

The source of sprouting beans for aduki is just the opposite. Small, round, shiny, deeply colored aduki beans imported from Japan or Taiwan and sold in Oriental food stores never sprout. Larger, oval, dull, lighter-colored domestic aduki beans from the health food store sprout better and are cheaper. Actually, domestic aduki beans are sometimes not aduki at all, but cowpeas. Pretend not to know the difference, because if you seek cowpeas in the health food store, you will find only aduki.

Guar beans are also accurately called brown mung beans. Occasionally health food stores stock these. While the germination rate is high, the beans that do not sprout remain as hard as pebbles and are not recommended.

Mung, aduki, and, if you insist, guar beans all sprout best with the least disturbance. Furthermore, they will grow profusely on the last half day if left unrinsed. For straight sprouts, grow these by the Towel or Tray Methods. Left unturned during the sprouting process, the sprouts grow long, straight, vertical roots. Roots always know which way is up—and down.

The Jar/Tube Method disorients the rootlets during the tumbling from rinsing and draining. Thus, you produce crooked sprouts. This affects neither their taste nor their nutrition, just their looks. The crooked man with a crooked stick who walks upon a crooked road which leads to his crooked house where he grows his crooked sprouts does not necessarily lead a crooked life, just an independent one, because the sprouts he eats he grows himself.

Crooked or straight, cooked or raw, mung and aduki taste good and are easily digested either way. But cooking is necessary to destroy natural toxins found in all beans, even sprouted beans. Mung and aduki sprouts in Asian cuisine traditionally are cooked. Indeed, most Americans first taste bean sprouts in stir-fried chow mein. Steaming also works well. If you are cooking a grain such as brown rice, add mung or aduki sprouts atop the rice during the last few minutes. If beans make rice nice, bean sprouts make rice twice as nice.

Lentils

Amount	¾ cup
Soak	5-12 hours
Rinse	2-3 times daily
Days	2-4
Length	¼-1 inch

Lentils, of all the beans, sprout the quickest and therefore the easiest. Their hulls do not require separation, their germination rate is high, and the few that do not sprout soften so that they need not be culled. Harvest lentils before the leaf appears on the third or fourth day. Leafy lentils are lentils past their prime.

Whether green or green-brown or brown when raw, most lentils are labeled simply lentils or green lentils. Whether green or green-brown when raw, both when cooked turn brown. Large green lentils are Laird, small green lentils are Eston, and really tiny black lentils are called French green. Are you confused yet?

Whether tiny crimson or medium red when raw, both these lentils when cooked turn pale yellow-brown. Whether crimson or red when raw and hulled, both when unhulled look brown. The lentil is red, but the hull is brown. Now that you surely are confused, have you given up on lentils altogether? Or have you given up lentils only for Lent?

Hulled red lentils pose still more riddles. Few batches sprout, because most hulled red lentils are split. With its protection removed, the germ flakes off and dies. Many batches of hulled but whole red lentils nevertheless have low germination rates. Batches that do mostly sprout will need many extra rinsings until the water runs clear. Yet red lentils that are unhulled and therefore look brown, not red, will not need extra rinsings. Got that? If so, go get red lentils. But don't expect red; they're orange.

Eaten in large quantities, raw lentil sprouts give some people gas, just as in any quantity, cooked unsprouted lentils give some people gas. But with cooked lentil sprouts there is usually no problem with this.

Cooking destroys the natural toxins in all beans. Sprouting neutralizes some of these toxins, but not all of them; cooking destroys the rest. Not surprisingly, most bean sprouts are unpalatable raw, but taste good cooked. Lentil sprouts taste good raw, but even better cooked.

Steam lentils for just ten minutes. After steaming, lentil sprouts sprinkled frugally with olive oil or vinegar or both make a simple main dish. Add herbs like basil or oregano, or spices such as cumin or caraway. You will likely be satisfied with a meal comprised solely of sunflower and lentil sprouts. The American Indians would have called it "Sproutatash."

Peanuts	
Amount	1 cup
Soak	8-12 hours
Rinse	2-3 times daily
Days	3-5
Length	¼-¾ inch

First, a comment from the peanut gallery: The peanut is a pea, not a nut, and the pea is a bean. So the peanut is a bean. Now you know beans about peanuts!

A second comment from the peanut gallery: Organically grown sprout seeds are always preferable to chemically grown, but organic peanuts are absolutely essential. Conventionally grown peanuts are often raised in fields whose alternate crop the previous year was cotton. Cotton is drenched in pesticides, which remain in the soil for next year's peanuts.

Unblanched raw peanuts sprout better than blanched, and the smaller, rounder Spanish (Valencia) peanut generally sprouts better than the larger, longer Virginia peanut. Whether you sprout the Spanish or the Virginia, do make sure the peanut is raw and its skin is tightly bound. Loose skins slip off during soaking, essentially blanching the peanut, allowing it to split and its germ to chip off.

The shell, distinct from the skin, presents a new set of parameters. A raw peanut in the shell is an easy nut to crack, so if available buy them unshelled. Shelled peanuts should be refrigerated.

Being peas, peanuts can substitute in recipes for chick-peas, yellow peas, and green peas. Unlike raw pea sprouts, raw peanut sprouts are quite digestible. Still, you should steam them for 10 minutes if you're going to eat them whole and for 15 minutes if you're going to grind them for hummus.

Despite all his innovations with peanuts, Dr. George Washington Carver somehow neglected to utilize peanut sprouts. You can now remedy his oversight, and you, too, can work for peanuts.

Chick-Peas, Green Peas, and Yellow Peas

Amount	1 cup
Soak	8-12 hours
Rinse	2-4 times daily
Days	2-4
Length	¼-½ inch

Chick-peas also are called garbanzo beans, but by either name are white. The black chick-pea, more accurately called "brown chick-pea" is a variety sold in Asian food stores under several names (few of which are "black chick-pea" or "brown chick-pea"). It is shaped like the Euro-Near Eastern chick-pea but is smaller, is less temperamental to sprout, and takes less time to cook.

Green or yellow peas, of course, must be whole, not split. Try sprouting split peas, and you will create a detestable split pea slime rather than the traditional split pea soup. Green and yellow, identical in their sprouting procedures, can be sprouted together in a colorful array.

Sufficient ventilation is crucial for successful sprouts of these peas. The Jar/Tube Method renders poor results with jars but good results with tubes. The Bag Method and certain commercial sprout containers work best. Peas provide good practice for sharpening your sprouting skills for the "big beans" to come.

Dry peas, after sprouting, regain the same taste and texture as fresh peas just out of the pod. Both must be cooked, preferably steamed, from 15 to 20 minutes.

Use these sprouts in any traditional recipe that calls for unsprouted peas. The quality of the dish with sprouts will improve remarkably. Hummus, for instance, is a dish made with ground chick-peas. Though ground sprouts lose their identity, the hummus gains a new one.

"BIG BEANS"
Anasazi, Black, Black-Eyed Peas, Great Northern, Kidney, Lima, Navy, Pinto, Roman, Soy, Turtle, etc.

Amount	¾ cup
Soak	8-24 hours (but change water after 12 hours)
Rinse	3-6 times daily
Days	2-4
Length	½-1½ inches (depends on variety)

Last and least, the "Big Beans" are different sprouters. They require more frequent rinsings and cooler temperatures than the other sprouts. And they must be cooked. In need of both cooling and cooking, they make perfect winter foods.

Challenge one confronting you is securing a source of dependable germinators. You may seek the ends of several rainbows and still not find your mason jar of gold. Commercially processed big beans often are treated precisely to inhibit sprouting, so of course, seek organically grown. Though untreated and very much alive, a specific organic variety still may prove a poor sprouter.

Among the dozens of varieties of soy, for instance, the best sprouters are Chief, Ebony, Illini, Lincoln, Richland, Peking, Cayuga, and Otoot. Knowing this, however, helps little. Few food distributors specify the variety but call all simply "soy." Fearns, the company which is to soy as Planters is to peanuts, does provide help to sprouts folks. Fearns packages and duly labels two types of soy: cooking and sprouting. Yet even Fearns neglects to name their particular variety of sprouting soy.

You indeed may possess a good germinator, but not yet know it. Thus, Challenge Two awaits you. Big beans, being big, require longer soaking times. While most will soften after soaking 12 hours, some require 24 hours. Just be sure to change the soak water after 12 hours.

Challenge Three is the sprouting technique. Big beans' need of ample ventilation disqualifies the jar of the Jar/Tube Method as a serious contender. The tube works well, the Bag Method better, and certain commercial containers best.

Challenge Four: The rootlet is very tender. If the rootlet breaks off, the bean begins to rot. Big bean, big stink. When employing the Bag Method, be gentle when immersing or handling the bag.

And Challenge Five: Big beans demand more frequent rinsings than other sprouts. The typical two or three times daily will suffice in cool temperatures. Otherwise, five or six daily rinsings are your only guarantee against rot. Certain commercial sprouting containers, however, which provide ample ventilation will enable you to keep big beans on the same timetable of two daily rinsings as your other sprouts.

Having persevered, you now have big bean sprouts. All beans contain both an enzyme that inhibits their digestion, and a complex sugar that promotes their fermentation. Hence the notorious, malodorous, musical gas in the gut. Sprouting breaks down the sugar, but does not entirely destroy the inhibitor. Cooking destroys the rest.

Steam the big beans at least 20 minutes. You can snip off the rootlet and eat that raw, but you must still cook the rest of the bean. And generally the bigger the bean, the smaller its rootlet.

Do big beans spell big troubles or just extra challenges? You are encouraged to disregard dietary dogmatism and to sprout for yourself all the big beans. Or you may wish to adopt the regimen of Pythagoras, the first famous vegetarian philosopher. Among his few surviving statements, his most memorable is: "Do not eat beans." Obviously he was ignorant of sprouting.

Radicle Vegetarian Recipes

Choose, Cook, Chop, Cheer

Eight out of ten Americans eat a diet primarily of flesh foods, fried foods, fast foods, and the four false foods of white flour, white sugar, white milk, and white salt. Seven out of ten adult Americans also eventually suffer from heart disease and cancer. Are these diseases linked to life-style and diet? You bet your life they are! If living like a couch potato does not kill you, eating chuck steaks will.

The first step off the fatal roller coaster ride of chronic illness begins with some knowledge of nutrition. Nutrients are classified into five groups: protein, fats, carbohydrates, vitamins, and minerals. Let's take a closer look at these through the microscopic lens of science.

Proteins consist of amino acids for building strong bodies 12,000 ways. The body digests food protein, breaks it down into building block amino acids, and then reconstructs the amino acids into body protein. Sprouting simplifies a seed's protein into amino acids, thus sparing the body the preliminary work.

Minerals form bone, teeth, hormones, blood, sweat, tears, and all sorts of other precious bodily fluids. Sprouting chelates (binds with amino acids) a seed's minerals into a more utilizable organic form so that the body does not "flush it all away."

Fats provide structure for cell membranes, insulation for body tissues, and energy for body warmth. Sprouting converts a seed's oils into more digestible polyunsaturated fatty acids, which the body is more prone to stoke as fuel rather than to store as fat.

Vitamins are catalysts that enable body cells to assimilate proteins, minerals, and fats. Sprouting increases two- to ten-fold a seed's many vitamins, especially its B vitamins. Two B or not two B, that is the question.

Carbohydrates (starches and sugars) fuel cell activity and muscle motion. Sprouting converts a seed's complex starches into simple sugars, again sparing the body the preliminary work. Devoting less energy to digestion, the body can direct more energy to running marathons, hiking mountains, or writing memoirs. Digestion is just digression.

Water is not a nutrient, but is second only to oxygen in its importance in maintaining life. It balances salts and acids in the body and transports nutrients. Water predominates in both the human body and the humble sprout. Humans must drink plenty of water, in addition to eating juicy fruits, leafy greens, or succulent vegetables, all foods that are soaked with water purified by the plants. Sprouts, too, are water purifiers. How to sprout? Just add water.

Nutrition class is now dismissed! More important than memorizing nutritional facts is knowing that nutritious whole foods put it all together for you.

Whole foods. Real foods. Health foods. Natural foods. Call it what you wish. Just be sure others have not done to it as they wish. Natural foods are grown without insecticides and chemical fertilizers, stored and shipped without fumigants and fungicides, prepared without preservatives, chemical processing, or mechanical refining—and eaten without fear.

Once you begin to eat in order to nourish the entire body rather than to titillate merely the tongue, only those foods that you know are good for you in turn will taste good to you. It is natural to like to eat and to like what you eat. It is equally natural to like to live and to like how you live. Eating natural foods, in part, contributes to living a naturally long and naturally healthy life.

Choosing

Few nutritionists agree upon what foods we should choose to eat. We can devote years to research on this crucial matter, or we can ignore all friendly advice and eat only natural foods. But by what definition is a food natural? Simply this: a natural food is one that appears on your plate in the same form as it appears in nature.

Procure food in season, locally, and organically grown

Sprouts that we grow at home, even in winter, fulfill the above three criteria. Upon harvesting our sprouts and transporting them over the long haul from the kitchen cabinet to kitchen table, we should observe at least two of these three criteria:

Prepare food fresh, raw, and whole.

Here then is my personal food grading system ranging from **A** ("Alive") to **D** ("Dead"):

A (all three criteria)	FRESH, RAW, and WHOLE
B (only two criteria)	not FRESH, or not RAW, or not WHOLE
C (one criterion)	only FRESH, or only RAW, or only WHOLE
D (no criteria)	not FRESH, nor RAW, nor WHOLE

I rate wheat sprouts an A (FRESH, WHOLE and RAW). Home-baked sprout bread, not being raw, rates B (FRESH and WHOLE). And whole wheat bread, from flour that is never fresh, rates only C (only WHOLE). But white flour Blunder Bread flunks out with D (not FRESH, nor RAW, nor WHOLE).

Obviously most sprouts achieve the high A mark. Even steamed sprouts at B (FRESH and WHOLE) score higher than their unsprouted forebears at C (only WHOLE), and B is good enough.

Cooking

Despite millions of cookbooks on the market, many people deny themselves the opportunity to eat truly high-quality food. Excessive and careless cooking reduces the nutritional value, taste, texture, and color of any food. Heat, if misused, is an artificial ingredient whose inclusion in any recipe can deplete rather than add to the quality of food.

Raw foods purists do not cook what can be eaten raw and do not eat what must be eaten cooked. Raw foods compared to cooked and sprouted foods compared to unsprouted are arguably more nourishing. Yet sproutarianism is not necessarily synonymous with strict raw foodism. You probably now eat many cooked foods—pasteurized fruit juices, baked breads, steamed vegetables, and boiled beans—and, certainly, many sprouts folks do, as well. Should you modify your diet to that suggested here, the presumable improvement in your health might be little affected whether you ate 80% of your diet from raw foods or 99%. In a 55 m.p.h. zone, the real risk of a speeding ticket begins at 65 m.p.h., not at 56. But some sprouts are more digestible, more palatable, and simply safer cooked than raw. Cook all beans that are sprouted, but first sprout all beans that are cooked.

Raw foodists can, of course, abstain from cooked bean sprouts such as inexpensive peanuts and instead eat uncooked but costly pine nuts. Such choices are a consequence of affluence. If pine nuts stretch the limits of your purse strings, you can simply eat pulse (bean) sprouts. Just take care to prepare your bean sprouts by the least deleterious means.

Low-heat slow cooking is less destructive than high-heat fast cooking. Sprouting "cooks" for three days with water and air what otherwise must be cooked for three hours with water and fire. If you must cook, steaming is preferable to boiling. Steaming requires a minimum amount of water and does not leech out the water-soluble nutrients that otherwise might be lost like a baby thrown out with the bath water.

Give a more natural foods diet a try. Throw your toaster out the window. Roll the stove and oven out the door. A single hot plate should suffice for steaming bean sprouts, for stir-frying clover sprouts, and for toasting tacos, pitas, or chapatis for sprout sandwiches. In the new empty space in the kitchen, install a stereo and listen to a symphony of sprouts. Beethoven beats ovens.

Chopping

Even with our full sets of teeth (and several sets of fillings?) we rarely chew our food thoroughly. Consider the blender a pre-masticative digestive aid.

The electric food processor is the modern miracle gadget that performs 1001 tasks—some well and some poorly. Unfortunately, manual appliances that very efficiently served single functions, especially where sprouts are concerned, are now forgotten. One of these is the manual food chopper (also called a meat grinder, perish the thought). A food chopper can grind dry what a blender only can liquefy and may give you better results in recipes where you just want to chop your sprouts, not turn them to paste. Secondhand food choppers often appear at garage sales at a fraction of their original price. Even when new, they cost only slightly more than electric blenders. Some recipes here require a blender, and a few specify a food chopper.

If you do not own a food chopper, alternatives exist. With labor, a wooden bowl and round blade complete the job. A small cylindrical contraption Grandma used for grating cheese or hardboiled eggs works too. Either of these will grind bean sprouts or nuts nearly as finely as a food chopper. But for grain sprouts, what then to do? Simply resort to your teeth, nature's own blender, juicer, and chopper. They're compact, portable, and cheap. In fact all nutritionists agree, if upon little else, that we should thoroughly chew our food.

Cheering

If you are eating sprouts, and lots of them, it probably means you are a vegetarian. Carnivores erroneously view vegetarianism as some great sacrifice. But scoring A hardly qualifies as sacrifice. Unfortunately, in many people's minds the label "vegetarian" defines only what you do NOT eat. The more accurate label "sproutarian vegetarian" explains also what you DO eat.

But by the time you finish pronouncing every syllable of "sproutarian vegetarian," your carnivore companions will have fallen asleep. The term "Radicle Vegetarian" surely will rouse them. Webster's defines "radicle" as the tender lower root portion of a sprout, the first growth of new life from the dormant seed. So the next time an acquaintance sees you eating sprouts and asks if you are a vegetarian, answer affirmatively, identifying yourself as a Radicle Vegetarian.

Down with vegetarian subtraction and renunciation! Up with sproutarian addition and affirmation! More varieties of sprouts abound than do different cuts of meats. And more kinds of sprouts flourish just from beans than there are species of farm animals. We more widely spread the message of vegetarianism with one good recipe than with all our philosophy. Three cheers for the Fresh, Raw, and Whole!

And onward with Radicle Vegetarian Recipes!

Sprout Salads

The difference is slight between mixing sprouts (on your plate) and sprouting mixtures (in your jar). Keep it simple, sprouthead! Load only as many distinct sprouts on the same plate as can stay separate. Otherwise the result is insulting to the sprouts and insipid for you. As in a Dagwood or foot-long sub sandwich, what contains everything tastes as nothing.

At the most, mix three. These can be either pre-mixed and grown together or post-mixed and thrown together. Any two sprouts on a single plate qualify as a "Success-through-Simplicity" sprout salad. More than two? Call that a "Success-through-Satiety" sprout salad. Either way proves successful, and this without the traditional lettuce, tomato, and cucumber.

So our first recipe contains a dozen other books' thousand other recipes. From its single page, you can extrapolate enough variety for a different salad every night for three years: 1001 Sproutarian Nights.

1001 Sproutarian Night Salads

Mix any of the following according to your taste or sprouting skill:

Alfalfa Sprouts
Clover Sprouts
Cabbage Sprouts
Turnip Sprouts
Broccoli Sprouts
Radish Sprouts
Mustard Sprouts
Lettuce Sprouts
Spinach Sprouts
Fenugreek Sprouts
Chia Sprouts
Cress Sprouts
Flax Sprouts
Psyllium Sprouts
Sunflower Sprouts
Pumpkin Sprouts
Almond Sprouts
Sesame Sprouts
Wheat Sprouts
Rye Sprouts
Triticale Sprouts
Buckwheat Sprouts
Rice Sprouts

Corn Sprouts
Popcorn Sprouts
Barley Sprouts
Millet Sprouts
Oat Sprouts
Quinoa Sprouts
Mung Sprouts
Aduki Sprouts
Lentil Sprouts
Peanut Sprouts
Chick-pea Sprouts
Green Pea Sprouts
Yellow Pea Sprouts
Anasazi Bean Sprouts
Black Bean Sprouts
Black-Eye Pea Sprouts
Kidney Bean Sprouts
Lima Bean Sprouts
Navy Bean Sprouts
Pinto Bean Sprouts
Roman Bean Sprouts
Soybean Sprouts
Turtle Bean Sprouts

Sprout Salad Dressings

A thousand-and-one salads easily expand into ten-thousand-and-ten by the mere addition of a dressing. Ideally, dressings are superfluous to an enjoyable meal, but realistically we enjoy their piquant flavor just the same.

Dressings, dips, sauces, and spreads—all are identical except for their thickness. Additional water or lemon juice transforms a dip into a dressing. Additional tahini or parsley transforms a sauce into a spread. Incidentally, buy dried parsley by the pound. Though almost tasteless, it adds texture and thickness, and is quite nutritious too.

Truth be told, parsley may be the only traditional ingredient for dressings found here. What our recipes do not include are salt, sugar, spices, garlic, onion, yogurt, cheese, tofu, miso, tamari, vinegar, and oil. Tahini and lemon juice serve as the sproutarian's oil and vinegar.

Only one natural foods company markets a raw tahini (sesame butter), and being the raw foods lover that I am, this is my personal preference. Lemon juice should be your own brand, freshly squeezed. When in season, lime is just as fine. Limes fit very nicely in the otherwise useless egg compartment of refrigerator doors. If you are out of both lemons and limes, oranges or grapefruit will do too. And if you wish to avoid citrus altogether, just add water.

No-Egg Mayo

This is the basic sauce for any need. Incredibly, adding water to tahini actually thickens it. Incredible or not, adding water makes tahini more digestible. Unlike other sprout dressings, this one requires no blender.

2 parts tahini
1 part water
1 part lemon juice
Dried parsley (optional)

Combine all the ingredients in a bowl or jar, and stir vigorously with a spoon. Add parsley if desired.

Variation: 2 parts water instead of lemon juice.

Avocado Creme

Yield: 1 quart

*Suitable for eating as is, this thick sauce deserves no seasoning.
If season you must, kelp and parsley will not overwhelm
the subtle taste of the avocado.*

4 medium avocados,chopped
2 cups water
½ cup lemon juice
2 Tablespoons kelp (optional)
¼ cup dried parsley (optional)

Combine the avocado, water, and lemon juice in a blender. Stir in kelp and parsley last, if desired.

Variation: Use carrot juice instead of water, and it will make this creme supreme.

Beet Red Beat

Yield: 2 cups

*Because most sprouts are green, brown, or white, this red dressing is
the perfect addition to an otherwise visually unexciting sprout salad.
Do not add any powdered herbs to this. Green mixed with red
equals brown—right back where we started.*

⅓ cup tahini
⅔ cup water
1 cup grated beets
½ cup ground ALMOND SPROUTS
¼ cup dried parsley
1 Tablespoon curry powder

Stir together the tahini and water, then combine in a blender
with the remaining ingredients.

Clover Cover

Yield: 1 quart

*Clover sprouts make an appropriate dressing for more clover sprouts,
and for any other sprout you might adorn.*

1 quart tightly packed CLOVER SPROUTS
½ cup lemon juice
½ cup water
2 celery stalks, coarsely chopped
½ cup tahini
1 Tablespoon fennel or anise seeds, ground
1 Tablespoon kelp

First combine the clover, lemon juice, and water in a blender.
Then add everything else and blend again.

Almond Sprouts Sauce

Yield: 1 quart

Any soaked nut can substitute for soaked and sprouted almonds. But this is a sprout book, not a soak book, so here we will stick to almond sprouts.

3 cups ALMOND SPROUTS
2 cups water
2 Tablespoons fennel, anise, or caraway seeds, ground

Combine in a blender until smooth.

Quick Nut Sauce

Yield: 1 quart

Use the nuts of your choice, raw of course. If you had not planned ahead and soaked nuts as required for the previous recipe, simply grind them dry as required here.

3 cups tomato purée (approximately 3 large tomatoes)
2 cups ground nuts
½ cup dried parsley
1 Tablespoon kelp

Blend enough fresh tomatoes in a blender to make 3 cups purée. Add the remaining ingredients and blend again.

Sprout Sandwiches

After we expand from unadorned salads to salads with dressings, we might consider sprout salad sandwiches. Sprouts as toppings to slices of bread amount to too much bread but few sprouts. It is better to use sprouts as stuffings. The receptacle to be stuffed might be any of these:

Whole wheat pita
Whole wheat chapati
Whole corn tortilla
Lettuce leaf, such as romaine
Nori sheet (sea vegetable wrapping for sushi)
Green or red pepper, halved

Spread a dressing onto or into the sandwich-to-be. Top that with a crunchy sprout, such as lentil or mung, which will adhere to the dressing. Then top the crunchy sprout with a leafy sprout like cabbage or clover. Curl the chapati, tortilla, lettuce leaf, or nori sheet, and the topping becomes a stuffing.

Of course, you may want to go all the way with your sandwiches, and spread your sprout toppings on sprouted bread. Here are two bread recipes for starters.

Undead Bread

Yield: two 9-inch plates or 1 cookie sheet

Considering all of the processing involved in milling flour and baking bread, it should be called the "chaff of life." This recipe is similar to the European "Vollkorn Brot" (whole kernel bread) which is surely the best of all baked breads. Ours is different because it is not baked, making it the best of all breads.

4 cups ground WHEAT SPROUTS
2 Tablespoons caraway seeds (optional)
1 Tablespoon kelp
2 Tablespoons tahini

The WHEAT SPROUTS must be finely ground (preferably twice) in a food grinder until they are the consistency of paste. Add the remaining ingredients and knead for a minute or two. Flatten on an oiled plate or cookie sheet. Dry under the sun in the summer or on top of a radiator in winter. Refrigerate before slicing.

Variation: 2 cups wheat sprouts and 2 cups rye sprouts instead of 4 cups wheat sprouts

Sprouted Bread*

This bread is unique. Anyone who has not tried it and is used to eating regular whole wheat bread or Wonder Bread (it's a wonder they call it bread!) is in for a surprise, because it is so different. Unlike traditional breads, sprouted wheat bread is moist and sweet. It is also much heavier and does not rise since it has no leavening.

Sprouted wheat bread is often called "Essene bread," named after the ancient Essene community in the Middle East that developed it. The sprouted wheat bread sold in stores is close to, but not quite true, Essene bread. Commercial bread is baked at around 250°F, whereas the Essenes never baked their bread; they just dried it in the sun.

This bread is unquestionably the most nutritious bread made. It is in a class by itself. It has more vitamins than other breads because the grains are sprouted. In two days of sprouting, vitamin A in wheat increases 50-75% and vitamins B1, B2, C, and E show significant increases. It also contains more fiber than whole wheat bread. These are the main reasons it has become such a popular item among health conscious people.

It is also the simplest bread, because it has only one ingredient: sprouted wheat (or a combination of sprouted wheat and other grains). It has no flour, oil, sweeteners, salt, leavening, or additives of any kind. When people first discover it, they often can't believe that it only has one ingredient.

1⅓ cups dry wheat berries = 3½ cups sprouts
= a one pound loaf of bread.

The five most critical factors in determining good sprouted wheat bread are:

1. the type of grain used,
2. the sprouting time of the grain,
3. the moisture content of the sprouts,
4. the grinding of the sprouts,
5. the baking.

Let's look at each of these factors in detail.

Type of Grain

The type of grain will not only determine the taste but also how well the bread holds together. Wheat, rye, and triticale are the three different kinds of grain that work the best. There are several different kinds of wheat all having their own distinct characteristics. Hard spring wheat has the highest gluten content and so makes the best bread. Soft winter wheat has less gluten. Bread made entirely from this type of wheat will not hold together very well, an important factor to remember. Rye has less gluten than spring wheat and rye sprouts have a higher moisture content. Bread made from rye sprouts alone will not turn out satisfactorily. Triticale is a hybrid cross between wheat and rye. It is very similar to wheat, but the properties will differ depending on where, when, and how it was grown. Use at least half hard spring wheat in all loaves of sprouted wheat bread. The only exception is for sprouted flat bread and crackers, where a higher percentage of winter wheat may be used if desired. Generally the soft winter wheat has a bit milder taste. Good combinations for the flat bread are half each of the two kinds of wheat or one-third of each of the two kinds of wheat and rye.

In addition to wheat, rye, and triticale, several other grains can be added in smaller quantities. Millet, short grain brown rice, hulled raw buckwheat, and whole hulled oats may be added in quantities not exceeding 20% of the total volume. It is important not to add in greater amounts than this, because they tend to make the bread fall apart. Their gluten content is low, and their moisture content is different. These grains are slower sprouters than wheat, and they have a much lower germination rate. They can, however, be added to sprouted wheat breads even if most of the seeds do not actually sprout. Like wheat, they should be used after only two days of germination. Many of these grains will start to go rancid if they are sprouted any longer. Do not attempt to get them to sprout by growing them for a longer time. It is best to sprout them with the wheat in the same container.

Remember, for the simplest and most foolproof bread use 100% hard spring wheat. These other combinations of grains are for variations after you have made successful batches of bread from hard spring wheat alone.

Sprouting Time

The length of time the wheat is sprouted is a critical factor. If the sprouts are grown for too short a period, they will be hard to grind, and the bread will be starchy and not as sweet. If they are grown for too long, they will be too moist and will have lost most of their gluten. In this case, the bread tends to fall apart and is extremely chewy.

Since sprouting conditions vary greatly depending on temperature and environment, it is best to use a visual examination of the sprouts as your guide to when they are ready to use. The longest of the thin roots should be 1½ to 2 times the length of the wheat berry. The thicker sprout shoot, which becomes the blade of grass, should be the same length as the wheat berry. The sprouting can take anywhere from 40 to 65 hours depending on conditions, including 8 to 10 hours of soaking time.

Moisture Content

The moisture content of the sprout grain is an important factor in producing a good quality bread dough. Properly sprouted hard spring wheat has a perfect moisture content.

For the best quality bread dough, the wheat should not be rinsed for 10 to 12 hours before the grinding. This dries out the wheat sprouts just enough to make a perfect dough. This little known secret makes a big difference. If the sprouts are rinsed within a few hours of grinding, it can mean a complete failure, because the dough will be too moist. Except for this 12-hour period just prior to grinding, the wheat should be rinsed three times a day.

Grinding

One sprouted wheat bread expert says that the fineness of grinding is the most critical factor of all. It certainly is one of the important factors. The more finely ground the sprouts are, the better the bread will be. If the sprouts are not ground well enough, the bread will not hold together. The dough may also end up having whole berries in it, which can become very hard on the outer crust.

There are several machines which can be used to grind the wheat. The best and easiest of all is the Champion juicer. Use the blank piece on the juicer in place of the screen and run the sprouts through once. If the cutter blades on your juicer are getting dull, you may want to run them through twice. Various electric food processors may also be used. Some work better than others, so you will have to do some experimenting if you have one. A cast-iron hand-crank food grinder also works well. You may want to put the sprouts through the grinder twice for a finer dough. Another machine which can be used is a castiron wheatgrass juicer. It works best if the screw piece at the end is either completely removed or screwed all the way out to the loosest setting. The white, glue-like substance that is formed in grinding the sprouts with hand crank machines should be added to the dough. Once the sprouts are ground into a dough, it should be kneaded by hand for a minute or two. Then form it into round loaves, 1½ to 2 inches high and 4 to 5 inches in diameter.

Baking

Traditionally, sprouted wheat bread was baked in the sun. In this way the maximum amount of nutrients were preserved, and the warm light energies of the sun were incorporated into the bread. In the summer months, you may wish to experiment with sun-drying your bread. If you do, or use a dehydrator, the loaves should be no more than ½ inch thick.

For most of us, the easiest and most convenient way to bake the bread is in the oven on ungreased cookie sheets. The main point to remember here is that the bread should be slow baked at a low temperature. It cooks from the outside in and you don't want to rush the baking. If it is baked at temperatures above 300°F, the outside will be too well done by the time the inside is done. Low-temperature baking also helps preserve some of the vitamins.

The highest temperature at which the bread should be baked is 250°F. At this temperature the inside of the bread will reach 175°F. On many gas ovens this is the lowest setting possible. For the size loaves previously mentioned, a baking time of 2½ to 4 hours is best. Smaller loaves take less time, larger ones more. Loaves should never be thicker than 2 inches or wider in diameter than 8 inches. If during the baking you would like to know if the bread is done, break it in half and check the center. If it is light colored and feels and tastes raw, it is not done. To help keep the bread from drying out too much during baking, place a pan of boiling water below the bread in the oven.

Many people wish to bake the bread at an even lower temperature to preserve as many nutrients as possible. The lowest setting on most electric ovens is between 125° and 150°F. The bread can be baked at this temperature for 6½ to 10 hours with equally good results. Baking a 1½-inch thick, 5-inch diameter loaf at 125°F for 8½ hours works well for me. With this method of baking, the internal temperature of the bread most likely reaches 115°F. Theoretically, this means some but not all of the enzymes would be preserved. Enzymes begin to be destroyed at 104°F and all of them are destroyed by 122°F. This, however, should not be of great concern if you eat plenty of fresh raw foods which supply an abundance of enzymes.

Variations

Once you have mastered the basic method of making the bread (which doesn't take long at all), you can start experimenting with adding herbs, chopped onion and garlic, grated vegetables, nuts, seeds, sprouts, and dried fruits to the bread dough. They should be added after the dough is ground and only in quantities of up to 15% of the total volume, so that the dough will hold together. If you plan to add extra ingredients, use only hard spring wheat berries for the bread dough, because they have the best gluten and moisture characteristics to hold the bread together. A good, high-protein bread can be made by adding a small amount of sprouted lentils or sprouted garbanzo beans to the bread dough. Here are some other ideas for variations: herb-onion-garlic, grated carrot with cinnamon, raisin-walnut, coconut-sesame-date, onion and soaked seaweed, and grated zucchini-spice. These are only a few suggestions out of thousands of possibilities.

A sourdough sprouted wheat bread can also be made. For this bread, just leave the raw loaves out in the open air for 24 hours. The bread will develop a sour taste. The loaves can then be baked as for regular sprouted bread. Another way, which preserves more enzymes, is to make thin loaves ¾ to 1 inch thick, and dry them in a food dehydrator for about 24 hours.

Sprouted wheat flat bread, chapatis, and crackers can be made by rolling the dough between two lightly floured plastic bags until ⅛ inch thick or less. Peel the dough off the bags, and dry in a food dehydrator, in the sun, or in an oven at 125°F until completely dry. To peel the dough off the plastic bags more easily, you may want to oil the bags lightly, then flour them.

If you sometimes wonder just how nutritious bread really is, wonder no more because this bread truly helps build strong bodies twelve ways!

Sunflower Cheese

Yield: almost 1 quart, depending upon the level of rising

When socialites imbibe wine, we can drink our grape juice unfermented. But when they combine wine with cheese, surely we would not wish to mix grape juice with milk. Instead we can ferment a batch of sunflower sprouts and create a feast of grapes and sunflower seeds fit for a gourmet.

3 cups SUNFLOWER SPROUTS
1 cup soak water
1 Tablespoon cumin
1 Tablespoon fennel (or caraway seeds or anise seeds)

Allow the soak water from the sunflower seeds to stand for 1 day while the seeds sprout. The liquid will slightly ferment when kept in the uncovered container at room temperature. Blend the SUNFLOWER SPROUTS, seasonings, and fermented soak water in a blender. Allow the batter to stand again in an uncovered container at room temperature for ½ to 1 day until it thickens and rises almost twofold. Oxidation causes the top of the cheese to turn black, but this is absolutely edible. Refrigerate.

❦

Sesame Cheese

Yield: 1 quart

Sesame Cheese is not fermented, so it is not really cheese. Still, Sunflower Cheese is to yogurt as Sesame Cheese is to ricotta. Either cheese may be spread on Undead Bread (page 101) or served as topping for any sprout salad.

2½ cups SESAME SPROUTS
1 cup ground almonds
2 cups water
1 juiced lemon
3 Tablespoons poppy seeds

Blend the SESAME SPROUTS and water in a blender. Add the remaining ingredients. If you would like a thicker consistency, add ¼ or ½ cup dried parsley. Refrigerate. After 1 hour this will acquire its cheesiness.

Hamlessburger

Yield: 1 quart (9 patties)

There's no herbs in this one. Their greenness would oppose the bright pinkness of the tomato and beet. The pink mixture looks exactly like chopped meat and the patty exactly like hamburger. Rest assured it tastes nothing like what it looks.

For sauce:

> ½ cup puréed tomato
> ½ cup tahini

> 2 cups chopped WHEAT SPROUTS
>   or RYE SPROUTS
> ½ cup LENTIL SPROUTS or MUNG BEAN SPROUTS,
>   chopped and cooked (steam for 10 minutes)
> ½ cup grated beets
> ½ cup grated carrots
> 1 cup ground walnuts or almonds

Stir the sauce ingredients together, and set aside. In a large bowl, mix all the other ingredients except the walnuts. Next, mix in the sauce. It really does cover everything if it is mixed thoroughly. Add the walnuts last and form the mixture into patties. Refrigerate at least an hour to become firm. Serve ungarnished.

Buckwheat Falafel Balls

Yield: 1 quart

This recipe tastes just like fried falafel, but it is not fried and it is not falafel. Falafel is made with either chick-peas or fava beans; this is buckwheat instead. If falafel is foreign to you, think of this as stuffing for your turkey-free Thanksgiving dinner.

2 cups BUCKWHEAT SPROUTS
1 cup water
1 cup grated carrots
1 cup dried parsley
¼ cup tahini
½ cup ground sesame or sunflower seeds
½ cup yeast flakes (optional)
1 Tablespoon vegetable seasoning or curry powder
1 Tablespoon thyme or marjoram
1 Tablespoon basil
1 Tablespoon kelp
½ cup ground sesame for rolling

Purée the BUCKWHEAT SPROUTS and water in a blender. Empty into a large mixing bowl, and add all the other ingredients. Mix well. Spread out no thicker than 1 inch on a cookie sheet or pie pan. Allow to dry under the sun in the summer or atop a radiator in winter for 8 to 10 hours. If you use the radiator, the room will fill with an aroma sweeter than any baked bread. Form into bite-sized balls, and roll in ground sesame. Or scoop slices out of the pan, and refrigerate. Serve in a bed of green leafy sprouts, topped with your favorite tahini sauce.

Variation: 2 cups raw buckwheat soaked several hours in 3 cups water replaces 2 cups BUCKWHEAT SPROUTS and 1 cup water

Aunt Una's Un-Tuna Salad

Yield: 1 quart (filling for one 9-inch pie or 9 patties)

The taste and color of the sunflower sprouts, the sea smells of the kelp and dulse, and the texture of the chick-pea sprouts all combine to resemble dark tuna.

½ cup CHICK-PEA SPROUTS

For sauce:

  1 cup water
  ½ cup tahini
  ½ cup ground flax

  1 cup chopped SUNFLOWER SPROUTS or PUMPKIN
    SPROUTS
  1 cup chopped CLOVER SPROUTS

  ½ cup grated carrot
  ½ cup diced celery
  ½ cup chopped dulse (first soak in water for 15 minutes)
  ½ cup parsley
  1 Tablespoon kelp
  1 Tablespoon rosemary
  1 Tablespoon fennel seeds
  1 Tablespoon vegetable seasoning

Steam the CHICK-PEA SPROUTS for 15 minutes; chop and set aside to cool. Stir together the sauce ingredients, and set aside. In a large bowl, mix the CHICK-PEA SPROUTS and all of the other ingredients. If the SUNFLOWER SPROUTS are dry enough, they may be ground in a blender or food processor rather than chopped. Thoroughly mix in the sauce. For patties, shape in the palm of your hand, roll in ground sesame, and refrigerate 1 hour before serving. Garnish with tomato slices and a thick sauce of your choice. This salad can be served as a spread on rolled-up romaine lettuce leaves or as a filling for pies, pressed into a shell of Wheat Sprouts Cookie/Crust (page 120).

Hummus

Yield: 1 quart

As the potato is to Ireland, the chick-pea is to Israel. And hummus is the mashed potatoes of the Middle East. For vegans it has become our butter and eggs. Indeed, its consistency resembles whipped butter and boiled eggs combined. Our blend contains neither garlic nor oil, two traditional ingredients, and of course no salt. What! Neither garlic nor oil? Hummus be kidding!

3½ cups CHICK-PEA SPROUTS or PEANUT SPROUTS
1 cup water from steaming
Juice from 2 lemons
1 cup tahini
1 cup dried parsley (optional)
1 Tablespoon curry powder
½ cup RADISH SPROUTS

Three-quarters of a cup of dried chick-peas sprouted in a 1 quart jar yields 2½ cups of CHICK-PEA SPROUTS, so put 2 jars into action for this recipe.

Steam the CHICK-PEA SPROUTS for 15 minutes. Blend the water from steaming, the lemon juice, and CHICK-PEA SPROUTS in a blender. Stir in the tahini alone, and you have a sauce for other sprouts. Thicken the sauce with parsley, and you have a treat of which one scoop is enough as a main dish. Either way, add the curry powder and RADISH SPROUTS.

Sprout Suppers

Sprout salads and sprout sandwiches may sometimes seem inadequate for festive events. On these occasions we can prepare complicated food extravaganzas. If you grow your own food, you will also probably want to invent your own recipes. The following recipes are intended more for inspiration than instruction. Indeed, implied in them all is the recommendation:

"EXPERIMENT!"

Sheepless Shepherd Pie

Yield: 1 quart (filling for one 9-inch pie or 9 patties)

Where there are no sheep, there need be no shepherd. Now that you mention it, this doesn't need to be a pie.

1½ cups CHICK-PEA SPROUTS or PEA SPROUTS

For sauce:

1 cup water
½ cup tahini
½ cup ground flax

1 cup chopped CABBAGE SPROUTS
  or CLOVER SPROUTS
1 cup chopped walnuts
1 cup grated daikon
½ cup ground sesame
½ cup parsley
1 Tablespoon kelp
1 Tablespoon curry powder
Ground sesame for rolling (optional)

Steam the CHICK-PEA or PEA SPROUTS for 15 minutes; chop and set aside to cool. (If the CHICK-PEA or PEA SPROUTS are dry enough, they may be ground in a blender or food processor rather than chopped.) Stir together the sauce ingredients, and set aside. In a large bowl, mix all of the other ingredients. Thoroughly mix in the sauce. For patties, shape in the palm of your hand, roll in ground sesame, and refrigerate 1 hour before serving. Garnish with tomato slices and a thick sauce of your choice. Can be served as a spread on rolled-up romaine lettuce leaves or as a filling for pies, pressed into a shell of Wheat Sprouts Cookie/Crust (page 120).

Succotash Patties/Pies

Yield: 1 quart (filling for one 9-inch pie or 9 patties)

One of the dishes Native Americans passed on to the rest of us immigrants is this combo of corn and beans.
Two ears yield a cup of corn in stereo.

1 cup LIMA BEAN SPROUTS

For sauce:
½ cup water
½ cup tahini

1 cup ground WHEAT SPROUTS
1 cup raw corn scraped from the cob
½ cup ground sesame
½ cup dried parsley
1 Tablespoon kelp
1 Tablespoon vegetable seasoning
Ground sesame for rolling

Steam LIMA BEAN SPROUTS for 20 minutes; mash and set aside to cool. (If the LIMA BEAN SPROUTS are dry enough, they may be ground in a blender or food processor rather than mashed.) Stir together the sauce ingredients, and set aside. In a large bowl, mix all of the other ingredients. Thoroughly mix in the sauce. For patties, shape in the palm of your hand, roll in ground sesame, and refrigerate 1 hour before serving. Garnish with tomato slices and a thick sauce of your choice. Can be served as a spread on rolled-up romaine lettuce leaves or as a filling for pies, pressed into a shell of Wheat Sprouts Cookie/Crust (page 120).

Curried Lentils

Yield: 1 quart

While curry powder is a candidate for use in almost any recipe, its color and texture complement lentils the best. You may wish to add more than a tablespoon. Just do not get curried away.

2 cups tomato purée
4 cups cooked LENTIL SPROUTS
¼ cup tahini
1 Tablespoon curry powder
1 Tablespoon kelp
½ cup chopped dulse (optional)

Blend enough tomatoes to yield 2 cups of purée, about 2 to 4 whole tomatoes. Pack the tomatoes into the bottom of the blender, and no other liquid will be needed. Add two cups of LENTIL SPROUTS, tahini, curry powder, and kelp. Blend again. Gently stir in the remaining LENTIL SPROUTS and dulse.

❧

Fenugreek Fix

Yield: 1 quart

This is really a recipe for a sauce, which incidentally, needs no blender. Its color and tang go well with fenugreek, but the sauce could very well be served atop something else.

3 cups FENUGREEK SPROUTS

For sauce:
1 cup yeast flakes
1 cup water
½ cup shredded coconut
½ cup dried parsley

Stir the sauce together, then add the FENUGREEK SPROUTS.

Middle Eastern Millet Mash

Yield: 1 quart

This cross (or crescent?) between tabouli and couscous is not only uncooked but also unprocessed—quite unlike those fractured wheat products. Speaking of wheat, ain't nothing here but us millet.

2 cups MILLET SPROUTS
1 cup chopped red or green peppers
1 cup grated carrot
½ cup dried (or 1 cup chopped fresh) parsley
1 cup No-Egg Mayo (page 97)

Mix all the ingredients. Serve in a rolled romaine lettuce leaf or pepper shell (red or green).

Variation: 1 cup MILLET SPROUTS and 1 cup chopped SUN-FLOWER SPROUTS instead of 2 cups MILLET SPROUTS

🌿

(Sprout, Not Split) Pea Soup

Yield: 1 quart

Soup is merely a dilute cousin of sauce, and sauce simply a sibling of dressing. So for a dressing, add one cup of water instead of two. Kelp is a delicious, nutritious sea vegetable and adds a salty flavor.

4 cups PEA SPROUTS, or 5 cups LIMA SPROUTS
2 cups water from steaming
⅓ cup ground sesame
2 Tablespoons kelp
2 teaspoons curry powder

Steam PEA or LIMA BEAN SPROUTS for 20 minutes; set aside to cool. Combine in a blender with 2 cups of the same water in which they were steamed. Stir in the other ingredients. Serve cool or warm.

Millet Matzoh

Yield: 1 quart batter (one 9- x 12-inch cookie sheet
or twelve 3- x 3-inch wafers)

When the ancient Hebrews left Egypt, they were too busy fleeing to sit around waiting for their bread to rise. So they simply left the yeast out of their recipe and invented matzoh. Of all our sprouted breads and wafers, this one made of millet tastes most similar to Moses' famous fast food—maybe the first fast food in history. Since millet is not glutinous like wheat and rye, flax is added to prevent crumbling.

3 cups MILLET SPROUTS
½ cup ground flax
2 cups water (preferably soak water from millet)
¼ cup poppy seeds

Blend MILLET SPROUTS and flax with water in a blender. This is most easily done in two batches. Add poppy seeds and mix well. Pour onto wax paper or lightly oiled pan. Dry under the summer sun or on top of the radiator in winter. Perforate into twelve 3-inch squares with a fork when still slightly moist. Cut the squares when crisp. Refrigerate before serving or these fragile wafers may crumble.

Sprout Slaw

Yield: 1 quart

Cabbage, being the hardiest of the leafy green sprouts, is the best one for any kind of slaw.

3 cups CABBAGE SPROUTS
½ cup grated carrots
½ cup diced celery
1 teaspoon kelp
1 teaspoon dill

For sauce:
⅓ cup water
⅓ cup tahini

Combine all the vegetable ingredients. Stir together the water and tahini, and combine with the vegetables. Serve on a bed of romaine lettuce.

Sprout Sweets

Neophyte vegetarians frequently suffer from gas. This malodorous malady occurs not from abstaining from meat but from replacing meat with indiscriminate combinations of every manner of fruit and vegetable. For instance, you might have grapefruit for breakfast (fruit), followed by granola (grains and dried fruit), mixed with bananas (fruit), and drowned in cow's milk (protein). This renewable source of natural gas, while solving the nation's energy crisis, will hardly enhance your social life.

If this is a problem for you, adopt a strictly natural hygienic regimen and don't combine fruits with grains, among other prohibitions and regulations. Sprouted grains combined with fruit, however, promise hope for the digestively disabled and a breath of fresh air for their unfortunate neighbors.

Girl Sprout Cookies

Yield: approximately thirty 1½-inch cookies

*This is the basic recipe for a sprout crust (page 120).
Unlike Wheat Sprout Cookie/Crust, this cookie is too
moist to mold into a crust. Being made from sprouts,
this is the most digestible cookie imaginable.
The flavor of raisins and the moisture of sunflower sprouts
combine for a taste like maple sugar
(without the maple sugar!).*

2 cups SUNFLOWER SPROUTS
1 cup ground raisins
1½ cups ground sunflower seeds
¼ cup flax

Knead all of the ingredients except the flax. Grind again to fully combine (this can be done in a food processor). Knead in the flax. Shape into balls and roll in coconut, or shape into cookies by flattening between wax paper. Allow to dry 1 hour before refrigerating.

Wheat Sprout Cookie/Crust

Yield: approximately thirty 1½-inch cookies or one 9-inch pie crust

Consider the Girl Sprout Cookie a preliminary rehearsal to this grand performance. From this recipe alone you can create enough variations to never experience the same show twice.

2 cups ground WHEAT SPROUTS
2 cups mashed dates
1 cup ground almonds
1 Tablespoon cinnamon or ginger
¼ cup ground flax (optional)

Knead all of the ingredients except the flax. Press again through the food grinder, or blend in a food processor to fully mix. Flax is optional because the WHEAT SPROUTS are glutinous enough to adhere everything into one piece, but if you prefer flax, knead it into the mixture now. Shape into bite-sized balls, and roll in coconut or ground sesame, or shape into cookies by flattening between wax paper. For a raw pie crust, press into a pie plate. Allow to dry 1 hour before refrigerating.

Variations: (1) Substitute RYE SPROUTS instead of WHEAT SPROUTS; (2) Use figs or raisins instead of dates.

Sunflower Sprout Creme

Yield: 1 quart

This is the perfect sauce to serve over a bowl of berries or sliced fruit. Peaches and whipped cream, strawberries and yogurt, blueberries and sour cream, bananas and cream—all foods of the past. Leave the cow out to pasture; fruit and Sunflower Sprout Creme is the food of the future.

4 cups SUNFLOWER SPROUTS
2 cups fruit juice
½ cup ground sunflower seeds
3 Tablespoons fennel or anise

Blend the SUNFLOWER SPROUTS and the fruit juice of your choice in a blender. If you don't use citrus juice, add the juice of one lemon, so the blended sprouts will not discolor. Add the remaining ingredients and serve atop fruit.

Apple Oats Apposed

Yield: 1 quart

Dr. Bircher-Benner takes the infamous credit for inventing muesli, the Swiss name for the fruit and oat breakfast cereal that has caused more vegetarian flatulence than all the baked beans in Boston combined with all the big apples in New York. Solution? Omit the milk, sprout the oats, and eat the apples fresh.

1 cup mashed dates
½ cup OAT SPROUTS or soaked whole oats
½ cup ground almonds
3 apples, chopped
Juice of 1 lemon

Combine the dates, OAT SPROUTS, and almonds in one bowl, and the apples and lemon juice in another. Mix the two together and serve immediately.

Sprout Shake

Yield: 1 quart

This tastes like pancake batter and maple syrup mixed together before hitting the frying pan. Add some carob for a chocolate flavor.

1 cup WHEAT SPROUTS
1 cup MILLET SPROUTS
1 cup soak water
1 cup fruit juice
2 bananas, cut in chunks

Soak the WHEAT SPROUTS in water for several hours in the refrigerator. Blend together all of the ingredients in a blender except the bananas. Add the bananas and blend again.

Variations: You can use RYE SPROUTS instead of WHEAT SPROUTS. They will not need soaking but will not be as sweet. Also, try 2 cups MILLET SPROUTS instead of 1 cup MILLET SPROUTS and 1 cup WHEAT SPROUTS.

🍂

Captain "Cooked's" Sweetwort

Yield: 1 quart

This brew saved British sailors from scurvy so they could pillage and plunder in good health. Although the captain called himself Cook, his crew was careful to steep, not boil the brew; otherwise most of the vitamin C would have been destroyed.

2 cups unhulled BARLEY SPROUTS
2 cups cool water
2 cups boiling water

Blend the BARLEY SPROUTS and the cool water in a blender. Add the boiling water and steep for several hours. Strain. If allowed to ferment, you have brewed beer. As it is, Sweetwort is sweet (what's in a name?) and non-alcoholic.

Wheatana

Yield: 1 quart

*"It sticks to your ribs," boasts the ads for flash-in-the-pan hot breakfast
cereals. "And in your intestines," they might add. By sprouting instead
of cracking the wheat, you can be sure that what goes in will come
out.*

4 cups WHEAT SPROUTS
1½ cups fruit juice
2 bananas
1 cup raisins
2 Tablespoons fennel or anise (optional)

Blend the WHEAT SPROUTS with the fruit juice in a blender,
then add the bananas and blend again. Add the raisins and fennel, if desired, and soak overnight in the refrigerator. The raisins
will absorb liquid and thicken the mixture in time for breakfast.
If you failed to plan your menu the evening before, gently heat
to make a thick and traditional hot breakfast meal.

*Variations: (1) Use RYE SPROUTS instead of WHEAT
SPROUTS; (2) Use chopped calmyrna figs instead of raisins.*

Safeguards Against Food-Borne Illness

While microbes on our foods usually are tasteless and odorless, they are not always inconspicuous. The 20 to 80 million cases of "food poisoning" that Americans suffer every year attest to the omnipresence of microbes.

Among many food-borne pathogens, E. coli commands much media attention for chronic beef recalls, but salmonella is the most common. The USDA admits that salmonella infects one in two chickens, one in seven pigs and steers, and one in twenty eggs, yet three out of four outbreaks of food-borne illness stem from salmonella in eggs, not in meat, because people often undercook eggs. Cooking destroys salmonella.

The lion's share of food-borne illness is borne by meat, milk, and eggs, so a sure way to reduce risk is to be vegan. A mere two percent of these microbes is borne by plant foods.

However, sprouts too have been linked to food-borne illness. Spanning three decades and stretching worldwide, outbreaks from sprouts are rare, but real.

All soils and all seeds naturally harbor fungi and bacteria. Most are harmless to animals, and some are even beneficial to plants, but a few are poisonous to humans. Microbes of all kinds flourish during the sprouting process because the same water and warmth that promote sprout growth also foster microbial growth. But salmonella and E. coli are microbes new to cultivated seeds, courtesy of modern animal agriculture.

E. coli, and especially salmonella, thrive in the intestines of factory farm animals, despite routine dosing with antibiotics. If the farm animal's manure is spread on a field as fertilizer, some of these microbes survive in the soil. During mechanized harvesting of sprout seeds, some of this soil gets stirred into the seeds. As you can see, the path of pathogens is often circuitous and sometimes calamitous.

Of all sprouting seeds, alfalfa seems most prone to contamination. This is perhaps due to scarification, a process that etches cracks into alfalfa seeds to enhance soaking and hasten germination. Distributors may discontinue this process because pathogens may anchor inside those cracks. Also, alfalfa may only seem more prone to contamination because more of it is eaten than other sprouted seeds, and it's always eaten raw. (Remember, cooking destroys salmonella.)

All raw foods pose a slight risk of food-borne illness. Fortunately, safeguards and solutions exist. Commercial sprout companies are sanitizing their seeds, knowing that any treatment which destroys pathogens on seeds also risks harming the seeds themselves. Methods of sanitizing seeds that safeguard viability include soaking in dilute solutions of chlorine, bromine, hydrogen peroxide, or acetic acid (vinegar); exposing to ozone, ultraviolet (UV) light, or heat (pasteurization); and, gasp, irradiation.

The Food and Drug Administration (FDA) favors irradiation but sprout folks do not. The FDA has approved chlorination, while the sprout industry hopes to gain approval for hydrogen peroxide diluted in hot water and for ozone treatment. Ozone assures the greatest safety all around, but its implementation is too complex for home sprouters.

Home sprouters can implement the "2% solution" of chlorination, though such a solution is quite strong. (Household chlorine bleach, for instance, consists of nearly 5% sodium hypochlorite.) Start with calcium (not sodium) hypochlorite, available from swimming pool, hydroponics, and, eventually, sprout seed suppliers. Mix 3 ounces (84 grams) calcium hypochlorite into 1 gallon (3.78 liters) of warm water. That's 20,000 parts per million (ppm), or 2 percent. Be careful not to inhale the chlorine fumes. Place the seeds in this initial soak water for 20 minutes. Remove the seeds, thoroughly rinse them in pure water, soak the seeds in pure water for several hours, and cap the leftover solution for future use.

Do home sprout folks really need to sanitize seeds? Yes and no. Fewer than one in 100 people who are exposed to food-borne pathogens actually show symptoms of illness. To assure a safe product for all, commercial sprout companies want to take precautions for not-so-healthy folks, notably infants, elders, and the chronically ill with weakened immune systems. But in healthy folks, stomach acids destroy most pathogens, and the rest of the digestive tract neutralizes the few acid-resistant unwelcomed guests that survive.

Which do you prefer in your food? Insects or insecticides? Fungi or fungicides? Bacteria or bleach? As a vegan on mostly raw foods, I have contracted food-borne illness several times but never from sprouts. But if suppliers were to offer "Certified Sanitized" seeds, I'd buy them.

Meanwhile, home sprout folks can observe some precautions. Illnesses have been traced to seeds from Africa, Asia, and Australia, so purchase domestic seeds whenever possible. Store the seeds in clean, dry glass jars. Thoroughly clean and dry all sprouting containers after each batch. Store raw sprouts in clean containers in the fridge chilled below 40°F (5°C). Rinse stored raw sprouts before serving. And enjoy!

Germination Termination:
A Mung Among Us

A meal comprised entirely of sprouts may be your idea of a feast and a delight, but the concept may not appear appetizing to your family and friends. Those who have yet to sample your fare often imagine a dark universe containing only two stars: alfalfa and mung. And among those who have tasted your banquet, how many have invited themselves back?

Your friends all appreciate traditional meals of familiar veggies. Many may even appreciate untraditional meals of familiar fruits. But your untraditional meals of unfamiliar sprouts will likely separate mere acquaintances from close friends.

Not that you should make friendships contingent upon your friends' acceptance or rejection of your sprouts. Mine are just observations of my past experience, not prognostications for your future experience. Some friends merely peck at the rich array of sprouts I serve for dinner. Before the meal is finished, they suggest going to the nearest vegetarian restaurant for dessert. At the restaurant, however, they order an entire meal. Occasionally, friends do eat all that I serve, right down to fenugreek and aduki sprouts. But rarely do they request a repeat performance. Farewell fenugreek. Adieu aduki.

Fortunately, new and lasting friendships do form and enrich our lives. Hurrah for sprouts, for sprout folks, and for friends of sprout folks! Some new friends can hardly wait to be invited back for another sprout feast. But wait they must—at least the three days necessary to sprout up another nutritional storm.

A most sensitive matter facing sprout folks is the date: not the fruit kind or the calendar kind—the people kind. On the first date with an available member of your preferred gender, you wisely become a closet sproutarian. Not because you sprout in a dark closet, but because you keep secret the fact that you eat lots of sprouts. Whole closets full! Given that your dating habits lean toward the vegetarians of our species, your discussion inevitably touches upon diet. Watch out! Do not dare let the cat out of the sproutbag. Wait until the second or third date, when you serve dinner at home.

Potlucks are a different story and "good-lucks" for some. At such gatherings, life as a mung bean among human beans is not difficult. Everyone, including you, can pick and choose. If you bring sprouts, few friends feel compelled to politely eat those on their plates, especially if they put none on their plates.

Potlucks among vegetarians are "best-lucks." The daring souls not only voluntarily eat sprouts, but often all the sprouts. Yet even among vegetarians the chances of finding a companion sprouter are slim. (Herein lies a definition of Companion Sprouting in addition to that listed on any sprout chart.) Consequently, you just may have to convert companions into sprouters. You might lend them this book with a bookmark coincidentally inserted at this page. And keep extra jars or tubes or bags on hand, precisely to give away to prospective companion sprouters. Then, when you tire of eating at home, you can eat at theirs.

One concluding admonition: Proper diet is only the third most important factor contributing to health. More important than diet is exercise, and more important than exercise is peace of mind. Better to share your friends' food than to separate yourself from them. Because what better way to achieve peace of mind than through love? And if indeed your loved ones eat your sprouts, then you are truly blessed.

Sprout Sources

Seeds, Beans, and Grains for Sprouting

You can purchase from your local natural foods store many varieties of seeds worth sprouting. In addition, mail order sources include these:

1) Especially for sprouts
2) Natural and organic foods
3) Gardening and farming

*Beginner sprout folks first sampling a variety need hardly more than one kilo or one pound. Reliable for highly viable and usually organically grown seeds, these five sources **especially for sprouts** provide the convenience of one-stop sprout shopping.*

Mumm's Sprouting Seeds
Box 268
Shellbrook, SK
Canada SØJ 2EØ [these are number zero's not letter O's]
(306) 747-2935 fax: (306) 747-3618
e-mail: mumms@sk.sympatico.ca
www.sprouting.com
14 BEANS, 7 GRAINS, 15 SEEDS

This list is not to be missed! A supplier to commercial sprouting companies, Mumm's also caters to individuals and welcomes American currency. High shipping costs to U.S. are offset by low seed prices.

The Sproutpeople
225 Main St.
Gays Mills, WI 54631
(877) SPROUTS; (608) 735-4735 fax: (608) 735-4736
e-mail: sprouts@sproutpeople.com
web: www.sproutpeople.com
14 BEANS, 6 GRAINS, 11 SEEDS

Also jar top lids; wheatgrass juicers; automatic sprouters; hemp sprouting bags; sprouting containers.

Hippocrates Health Institute
1443 Palmdale Court
West Palm Beach, FL 33411
(561) 471-8876 fax: (561) 471-9464
e-mail: hippocrates@worldnet.att.net
web: www.hippocratesinst.com
5 BEANS, 5 GRAINS, 9 SEEDS

Also books; one-week residency programs; wheatgrass juicers; automatic sprouters; cafeteria trays for the Soil Method. A great sprout source!

Sprout House (Sproutman)
17267 Sundance Dr.
Ramona, CA 92065
(800) SPROUTS; (760) 788-4800 fax: (760) 788-7979
e-mail: info@sprouthouse.com
web: www.SproutHouse.com
4 BEANS, 4 GRAINS, 8 SEEDS

Also books; wheatgrass juicers; linen sprouting bags and bamboo basket kits.

International Specialty Supply (ISS)
820 East 20th St.
Cookeville, TN 38501
(931) 526-1106, ext.106 for retail orders; fax: (931) 526-8338
e-mail: sprouts@infoave.net
web: www.ucbd.com/iss/sprouts.htm
7 BEANS, 1 GRAIN, 6 SEEDS (USUALLY NOT ORGANIC)

The major supplier of hi-tech equipment and packaging supplies to commercial sprouting companies, ISS issues no catalog for retail sales of seeds; nonetheless they welcome your order, so contact them for current price quotes.

Most seeds from your local natural foods store are intended for cooking and eating, not necessarily for soaking and sprouting. Consequently, due to age or improper storage, viability can be inconsistent. Among mail order distributors of **natural and organic foods**, these two are most responsive to the needs of fastidious sprout folks, and Jaffe Brothers especially of frugal sprout folks. Both also offer sprouting containers and kits.

Jaffe Brothers Natural Foods
P.O. Box 636
Valley Center, CA 92082-0636
(760) 749-1133 fax: (760) 749-1282
e-mail: jb54@worldnet.att.net
17 BEANS, 18 GRAINS, 13 SEEDS

Also unblanched and raw peanuts and almonds. All in 2-, 5-, and 25-pound quantities—whole foods at wholesale prices.

Garden Spot (Shiloh Farms)
438 White Oak Rd.
New Holland, PA 17557
(800) 829-5100; (717) 354-4936 fax: (717) 354-4934
e-mail: grdnspot@ptd.net
34 Beans, 22 Grains, 7 Seeds

All in 1 and 25 pound quantities.

Mail order sources for **gardening and farming** seeds number in the hundreds, but only a handful offer untreated seeds in bulk quantities. Untreated and bulk, that's the winning combo!

Unless their catalog states otherwise, gardening seeds are routinely treated with fungicides, and sometimes also with insecticides. That poses little health risk if the seed starts small, if the plant grows big, and if the growing season stretches long. For sprouting, however, beware! Another warning: Even if from untreated seeds, the plants themselves and therefore the sprouts of the nightshades (a family with members such as belladonna and tobacco) are toxic. So do not sprout the seeds of tomatoes, eggplants, and peppers.

An ever-present consideration is cost. Small packets suffice for gardeners tending a single row all season long in their backyards, but for sprout folks that's enough for only a single tray for one week on a window sill. For "dirt cheap" seeds, seek bulk quantities by the kilo or pound. That levels the planting field to just four sources. Though not always organically grown, seeds from these four sources will expand your repertory into a preponderance of sprouts.

Fedco
P.O. Box 520
Waterville, ME 04903-0520
23 BEANS, 4 GRAINS, 33 SEEDS
From $3 to $12 per pound, with hundreds more seeds at more cost; seed orders accepted only from November to March; send $2 for their very interesting seeds (specify seeds) catalog.

Ornamental Edibles
3622 Weedin Ct.
San Jose, CA 95132
web: www.ornamentaledibles.com
33 SEEDS
From $5 to $20 per pound, with dozens more seeds at more cost; the definitive seed source for mesclun salad greens, both mixes and individual greens. Send $2 for their very informative catalog.

Johnny's Selected Seeds
1 Foss Hill Rd
Albion, ME 04910-9731
(207) 437-4301
fax: (800) 437-4290; (207) 437-2165
e-mail: homegarden@johnnyseeds.com
web: www.johnnyseeds.com
42 BEANS, 11 GRAINS, 27 SEEDS
From $5 to $14 per pound, with dozens more seeds at more cost; Johnny's provides both treated and untreated seeds; be sure to specify untreated.

Vermont Bean Seed Company
business office:
Fair Haven, VT 05743-0250
(802) 273-3400
fax: (888) 500-7333
125(!) BEANS

shipping office:
Vaucluse, SC 29850-0150
(803) 663-0217

Most cost $5 per pound, from $15 to $19 per 5 pounds, from $27 to $30 per 10 pounds.

Commercial Containers and Jar Top Lids

The trusty Mason jar, available anywhere locally, is a do-it-yourself sprouting container better than most commercial ones. Its lid, however, is improved when made of plastic. Jar top plastic lids are available from Jaffe Brothers (page 130), Sproutpeople (page 129), and Sprout Ease (page 132). And in "The Tube," two lids are better than one.

Among many other commercial sprouting containers, bags made from linen or hemp work well, especially for the big beans. You can order linen bags from Sprout House (page 130) and hemp bags from Sproutpeople (page 129). This author's own choice for bountiful big beans is the Sproutamo "Easy Sprout," conceived by an engineer who attests the idea came to him in a dream. Sprouting is believing!

Sproutamo
P.O. Box 17
Lake Mills, WI 53551
(920) 648-3853 fax: (920) 648-2115
e-mail: ezsprout@gdinet.com
"Easy Sprout," probably the best and certainly the most convenient (easy!) commercial container; available in 1-, 3-, 6-, and 12-packs; or singly by special order from most health food stores.

Sprout-Ease
P.O. Box 769
Kerrville, TX 78028-0769
(830) 896-0117
Jar top plastic lids in three meshes; also, "The Tube," a well-ventilated tube with lids at both ends.

Both the lids and "The Tube" are available by special order from most health food stores.

Planting Trays

Cafeteria trays, though synthetic, are perfect for the down-to-earth and back-to-land Soil Method. These are available from Hippocrates Health Institute (page 129) or from any restaurant supplies store.

Automatic Sprouters

Self-rinsing, electrical-powered systems oppose the sproutarian self-sufficient, low-tech ideal. But some cottage industry folks spread sprouts around town to local restaurants and health food stores. Automatic sprouters are useful for bulk sprouting. The "Mist-A-Ponic" in one, two, or three tiers is available from Sproutpeople (page 129), Hippocrates Health Institute (page 129), and Ann Wigmore Foundation (page 134).

Creative Craftsman
38 14th St, BHR
Okeechobee, FL 34974
(941) 467-6696
web: www.autosprout.com
Four models; demonstration video available.

Literature

Hippocrates Health Institute (page 129) offers books by Wigmore, Kulvinskas, Cousens, Clement, and others. In addition, you can get your information straight from the sprout scouts.

Sprouting Publications
P.O. Box 62
Ashland, OR 97520
(541) 488-2326 fax: (541) 488-4429
voice-mail: (800) 746-7413
e-mail: lolaroja@aol.com
Books by radicle vegetarian Mark Braunstein; complete 45-issue set of the seminal **Sprout Letter***, published between 1980 and 1991; also, the "Sprout Chart," a laminated poster from which this book's grow charts are adapted.*

Sproutman Publications (Sprout House)
P.O. Box 1100
Great Barrington, MA 01230
(413) 528-5200 fax: (413) 528-5201
e-mail: sprout@sproutman.com
web: www.Sproutman.com
Books by Sproutman Steve Meyerowitz.

Twenty-First Century Publications
P.O. Box 702
Fairfield, IA 52556
(800) 593-2665; (515) 472-5105
e-mail: books21st@aol.com
Books by sprout boy scout Viktoras Kulvinskas and others.

Ann Wigmore Foundation
P.O. Box 399
San Fidel, NM 87049
(505) 552-0595; (505) 384-1017
e-mail: wigmore@wigmore.org
web: www.wigmore.org

Books by sprout girl scout Ann Wigmore and others; wheatgrass juicers; automatic sprouters—mainland contact for information on residency programs in Puerto Rico at Ann Wigmore Institute. P.O. Box 429, Rincon, PR 00677 (phone 787-868-6307).

International Sprout Growers Association (ISGA)
P.O. Box 270
Marion, MA 02738-0270
(800) 448-8006; (413) 253-8965; (508) 763-2714
fax: (413) 253-6965; (508) 763-3316
web: www.isga-sprouts.org

Semi-annual **Sprouter's Journal**, *which addresses concerns of commercial sprouting companies; affiliate membership for non-professionals who only dream about sprouting for a living.*

Index

Sprout-at-a-Glance Chart*

Seeds	Method	Amount Jar/Tube (1 quart)	Soak Hours	Temp. °F
Aduki Bean	Jar/Tube - Bag	½ cup	5 - 10	65 - 85
Alfalfa	Jar/Tube - Bag Tray	2 Tablespoons	3 - 6	60 - 85
Almond	Jar/Tube - Bag Towel	2 cups	10 - 12	70 - 85
Barley[1]	Jar/Tube - Bag	1½ cups	6 - 10	68 - 80
Broccoli	Jar/Tube - Bag Soil	3 Tablespoons	3 - 6	65 - 85
Buckwheat	Jar/Tube - Bag	1 cup	15[2] minutes	60 - 85
Buckwheat Unhulled	Soil	—	8 - 14	65 - 85
Cabbage	Jar/Tube - Bag	3 Tablespoons	4 - 8	60 - 85
Chinese Cabbage	Jar/Tube - Bag	3 Tablespoons	3 - 6	65 - 85
Chia	Clay Saucer	—	—	65 - 85
Clover (Crimson)	Jar/Tube - Bag Tray	2 Tablespoons	3 - 6	60 - 85
Corn	Jar/Tube - Bag	1½ cups	10 - 14	68 - 85
Popcorn	Jar/Tube - Bag	1½ cups	10 - 14	68 - 85

* ©1993 by Sprouting Publications (Original Sprout Chart available, see page 133.)
[1] Viable seed not readily available. Maybe used even if no sprout appears.
[2] Soak no longer than 15 minutes, then rinse hourly for 4 hours, then 2-3 times per day.

Rinses per Day	Days	"Green" on Last Days	Inches	Uses
3 - 5	2 - 4		½ - 1½	Salads - Main Dishes Sandwiches
2 - 3	4 - 6	Yes	1½ - 2	Salads - Main Dishes Sandwiches - Drinks - Dressings
2 - 3	1 - 2		0 - ⅛	Salads - Main Dishes - Drinks Breads - Desserts - Dressings
2 - 3	1 - 2		0 - ¼	Salads - Main Dishes - Breads
2 - 3	3 - 10	Yes	1 - 1½	Salads - Sandwiches Cole Slaw
2 - 3	2 - 3		½ - 1	Salads - Sandwiches - Garnish
—	8 - 15		4½ - 6	Salads (excellent lettuce substitute)
2 - 3	3 - 5	Yes	1 - 1 ½	Salads - Sandwiches - Soups Cole Slaw
2 - 3	4 - 5	Yes	1 - 1½	Salads - Sandwiches - Soups Cole Slaw
—	3 - 5	Yes	1 - 1½	Salads - Garnish
2 - 3	4 - 6	Yes	1½ - -2	Salads - Casseroles - Breads Sandwiches - Soups
2 - 3	2 - 3		¼ - ½	Main Dishes - Soups - Breads Cereals - Granola
2 - 3	2 - 3		¼ - ½	Main Dishes - Soups

Seeds	Method	Amount Jar/Tube (1 quart)	Soak Hours	Temp. °F
Cress	Clay Saucer	—	—	50 - 72
Fenugreek	Jar/Tube - Bag Soil	¼ cup	4 - 8	65 - 85
Flax	Clay Saucer	—	—	65 - 85
Garbanzo Bean	Jar/Tube - Bag	1 cup	8 - 12	68 - 85
Kidney Bean	Jar/Tube - Bag	¾ cup	8 - 12	68 - 85
Lentil	Jar/Tube - Bag	¾ cup	5 - 8	60 - 85
Lettuce	Jar/Tube - Bag Soil	3 Tablespoons	0	65 - 85
Millet[1]	Jar/Tube - Bag	1½ cups	5 - 7	70 - 80
Mung Bean	Jar/Tube - Bag	⅓ cup	5 - 10	68 - 85
Mustard	Jar/Tube - Bag Soil	3 Tablespoons	4 - 6	65 - 85
Oat[1]	Jar/Tube - Bag towel	1½ cups	3 - 5	68 - 80
Pea	Jar/Tube - Bag Soil	1 cup	7 - 10	
Peanut	Jar/Tube - Bag	1 cup	8 - 12	68 - 85
Pinto Bean	Jar/Tube - Bag	¾ cup	8 - 12	68 - 85

[1] Viable seed not readily available. May be used even if no sprout appears.

Rinses per Day	Days	"Green" on Last Days	Inches	Uses
—	4 - 5	Yes	1 - 1½	Salads - Spicy Garnish Sandwiches
2	3 - 6	Yes	1 - 2	Salads - Main Dishes
—	0 - 5	Yes	1 - 1½	Salads - Drinks
3 - 4	2 - 4		½	Salads - Main Dishes - Dips
3 - 4	2 - 4		½ - 1	Main Dishes - Soups
2 - 3	2 - 4		¼ - 1	Salads - Main Dishes - Breads Loaves - Soups - Sauces - Dips
2 - 3	4 - 5	yes	1 - 1½	Spicy Garnish
2 - 3	1 - 2		0 - ⅛	Salads - Main Dishes - Soups Breads - Cereals
3 - 5	3 - 5		1 - 3	Salads - Main Dishes - Soups Loaves - Drinks - Sandwiches
2 - 3	4 - 5	Yes	1 - 1½	Salads - Soups - Garnish Sandwiches - Juicing
1 - 2	1 - 2		0 - ¼	Salads - Main Dishes - Soups Breads - Cereals
2 - 3	2 - 3	yes	¼ - ½	Salads - Main Dishes - Soups Dips
2 - 3	3 - 5		¼ - ¾	Main Dishes - Soups
3 - 4	3 - 4		½ - 1¼	Main Dishes - Dips

Seeds	Method	Amount Jar/Tube (1 quart)	Soak Hours	Temp. °F
Psyllium	Clay Saucer	—	—	65 - 80
Pumpkin	Jar/Tube - Bag	1½ cups	4 - 6	65 - 85
Quinoa	Jar/Tube - Bag	⅓ cup	2 - 4	55 - 80
Radish	Jar/Tube - Bag Soil	3 Tablespoons		60 - 85
Rice	Jar/Tube - Bag	1½ cups		55 - 80
Rye	Jar/Tube - Bag Soil	1 cup		50 - 72
Sesame	Jar/Tube - Bag	2 cups		68 - 80
Soybean	Jar/Tube - Bag	¾ cup		65 - 85
Spinach	Jar/Tube - Bag Soil	3 Tablespoons		65 - 85
Sunflower	Jar/Tube - Bag	1 cup		60 - 80
Sunflower Unhulled	Soil	—		60 - 80
Triticale	Jar/Tube - Bag Soil	1 cup		60 - 80
Turnip (and Rutabaga)	Jar/Tube - Bag Soil	3 Tablespoons		65 - 85
Wheat	Jar/Tube - Bag Soil	1 cup		55 - 80

Rinses per Day	Days	"Green" on Last Days	Inches	Uses
—	4 - 5	Yes	¾ - ½	Drinks - Garnish
2	0 - 2		0 - ⅛	Main Dishes - Sauces - Dips
2 - 3	1 - 4	Yes	¼ - 1¼	Salads - Main Dishes - Cereals
2 - 3	4 - 5	Yes	1 - 2	Salads - Soups - Sandwiches Dips - Hot Spice
2 - 3	1 - 3		0 - ⅛	Main Dishes - Soups
2	2 - 3		¼ - ½	Salads - Soups - Breads Cereals - Granola
3 - 4	1 - 2		⅛	Salads - Main Dishes - Cereals Breads - Desserts
3 - 4	3 - 4		½ - 2	Salads - Main Dishes - Soups Breads
2 - 3	3 - 6	Yes	1 - 2	Salads - Garnish
2	1 - 3		0 - 1	Salads - Soups - Breads - Dips Sauces - Dresssings - Cereals
—	8 - 9	Yes	3 ½ - 6	Salads - Juicing
2	2 - 3		¼ - ½	Salads - Soups - Breads Desserts - Cereals - Granola
2 - 3	3 - 5	Yes	1 - 1½	Salads - Sandwiches
2	2 - 3		¼ - ½	Salads - Soups - Breads Juicing - Desserts - Granola

Look for these other books at you local bookstore or you can order directly from the publisher. Call for free catalog.

Book Publishing Co.
P.O. Box 99
Summertown, TN 38483
800-695-2241

Vegetarian Resource
Directory
$9.95

The Shiitake Way
$9.95

New Farm Vegetarian
Cookbook
$9.95

Tasty Bytes
Cookbook
$9.95

Nutritional Yeast
Cookbook
$9.95

Soyfood Recipes for
the American Table
$9.95

Please add $2.50 each book
for shipping and handling.